# CHOOSING THE
# DREAM

**Recent Titles in**
**Contributions to the Study of Religion**

# CHOOSING THE DREAM

## THE FUTURE OF RELIGION IN AMERICAN PUBLIC LIFE

### Frederick Mark Gedicks
AND
### Roger Hendrix

CONTRIBUTIONS TO THE STUDY OF RELIGION,
NUMBER 32
Henry Warner Bowden, *Series Editor*

GREENWOOD PRESS
New York • Westport, Connecticut • London

**Library of Congress Cataloging-in-Publication Data**

Gedicks, Frederick Mark.
    Choosing the dream : the future of religion in American public
life / Frederick Mark Gedicks, Roger Hendrix.
        p.   cm.—(Contributions to the study of religion, ISSN
0196–7053 ; no. 32)
    Includes bibliographical references and index.
    ISBN 0–313–27809–1 (alk. paper)
    1. United States—Religion—1960–  I. Hendrix, Roger.
II. Title.  III. Series.
BL2525.H45   1991
200′.973′09045—dc20        91–10426

British Library Cataloguing in Publication Data is available.

Library of Congress Catalog Card Number: 91–10426
ISBN: 0–313–27809–1
ISSN: 0196–7053

First published in 1991

Greenwood Press, 88 Post Road West, Westport, CT   06881
An imprint of Greenwood Publishing Group, Inc.

Printed in the United States of America

The paper used in this book complies with the
Permanent Paper Standard issued by the National
Information Standards Organization (Z39.48–1984).

10 9 8 7 6 5 4 3 2 1

**Copyright Acknowledgments**

Gedicks & Hendrix, "Democracy, Autonomy, and Values: Some Thoughts on Religion and Law in Modern America," 60 *S. Cal. L. Rev.* 1579–1619 (1987), reprinted with the permission of the *Southern California Law Review*.

Frederick M. Gedicks, "Toward a Constitutional Jurisprudence of Religious Group Rights," 1989 *Wis. L. Rev.* 99–169. Reprinted with permission of the *Wisconsin Law Review*; University of Wisconsin, copyright owner.

Gedicks, "The Religious, the Secular, and the Antithetical," 20 *Capital Law Review* 113–45 (1991), reprinted with permission of the *Capital Law Review*.

Gedicks, "Some Political Implications of Religious Belief," *Notre Dame Journal of Law, Ethics & Public Policy* 4 (1989): 419–49, reprinted with permission of the *Notre Dame Journal of Law, Ethics & Public Policy*.

To Cheryl
and
Nicea Ann

A culture without dreams is finished.

—Joseph Campbell

The day shall come when I will pour out my spirit on all mankind; your sons and your daughters shall prophesy, your old men shall dream dreams and your young men see visions.

—Joel 2.28

# Contents

# Preface

Religion has been deeply embedded in the history and culture of the United States from its birth. During the 20th century, however, portions of American society have attempted to disengage themselves from religion, resulting in a fascinating and puzzling contradiction: American public life has grown increasingly secular, while American private life has remained deeply committed to religious belief and experience. This contradiction is the focus of this book.

This book itself represents a contradiction of sorts. The proper place of religion in American public life is a controversial issue that has been significantly affected by intellectual developments in many academic disciplines. Although academics are no doubt generally familiar with these developments, many people outside of academic communities are not. It was our goal to write a book that would serve to introduce nonacademics to this area. Accordingly, we attempted to write the text in a style that is accessible to the student and the general reader. We have taken pains to define terms that may seem self-evident to those familiar with these issues. We also have dispensed with textual notes, and generally have used notes only for quoted and statistical material. We have, however, included a bibliography of our principal source materials. Despite these accommodations to the general reader, we nevertheless hope that academics as well will find the book useful.

Many people helped us in writing this book, but several deserve particular thanks. Jack Adamson, Mark Bench, and John Singleton provided important suggestions and encouragement at the initial stages of the project, without which we might never have undertaken it. Katherine Durant contributed insights drawn from parallel research she was engaged in at the time we generated the first draft, and loaned us her father's Bible as well. Richard Campbell, Richard Carmickle, David Grindle, Mark Peterson, and Larry Stewart provided invaluable research assistance at various stages of the project. Nancy Ehrenreich, Jim Gordon, Steve Smith, Cari Updike, and Paul Updike read the entire manuscript and offered many helpful comments and criticisms. Finally, Professor Gedicks wishes to acknowledge travel support from the Mercer University School of Law during the summer of 1988, and research support from the University of Denver College of Law during the 1989–90 academic year.

Parts of this project were originally published or presented elsewhere in somewhat different form. The book itself grew out of an essay which we co-authored several years ago: Gedicks and Hendrix "Democracy, Autonomy, and Values: Some Thoughts on Religion and Law in Modern America," *Southern California Law Review* #60 (1987): 1579–1619. Parts of that essay appear in Chapters 1, 2, 5, 6, 7, and 9, and are reprinted with the permission of the *Southern California Law Review*. Chapter 10 and part of Chapter 9 were included in Gedicks, "Toward a Constitutional Jurisprudence of Religious Group Rights," *Wisconsin Law Review* 1989: 99–169, and Chapter 3 and part of Chapter 8 were included in Gedicks, "The Religious, the Secular, and the Antithetical," *Capital Law Review* 20 (1991): 113–45. Chapter 4 and parts of Chapters 5 and 11 first appeared as Gedicks, "Some Political Implications of Religious Belief," *Notre Dame Journal of Law, Ethics & Public Policy* 4 (1989): 419–49. We gratefully acknowledge permission from the copyright holders to reprint these works. Finally, portions of Chapters 1 and 2 were presented by Dr. Hendrix as part of a lecture series entitled "Social, Political, and Economic Trends in the 21st Century," delivered during 1989 and 1990 to the Strategic Planning Conference of the American Bankers Association and to various state banking organizations.

# CHOOSING THE DREAM

# Introduction: Religion in American Public Life

Religious movements have been a constant of American history. By some counts, we have experienced four major periods of religious revival. The "First Great Awakening" in the early 18th century firmly established Protestantism as the American theology. The "Second Great Awakening" at the outset of the 19th century brought forth a revitalized, evangelical Protestantism that deeply influenced American culture throughout that century. The temperance movement at the dawn of the 20th century, part of the larger Progressive movement in American politics, is sometimes referred to as the "Third Great Awakening." It was an ambitious attempt to recommit the United States to evangelical Christianity in the face of the challenges brought on by industrialization and modernization.

The last 20 years have seen still another revival of religion, which some have styled the "Fourth Great Awakening." This latest turn to religion has uncovered and sharply defined a cultural paradox that has been evident in the United States for some time. Large numbers of Americans—a majority, by some measures—are deeply religious in their personal lives, yet American public life is largely empty of religious content and often hostile to religion. Notwithstanding persistent attempts by some to inject religion into public life, the custodians of that life, the practitioners of so-called "elite culture" in politics, government, law, education, media, and the arts, have little understanding of religion except as a personal and private phenomenon. The consequences of this paradox are serious and far-reaching, but only in the last decade have Americans begun to take note of them.

There is a gap between what Americans would like to be, and what, in fact, they are. What Americans want for the United States, and for their communities, their families, and themselves, simply does not match the reality of American life. As cities and schools descend into a quagmire of crime and gangs, drugs and disease, Americans see the possibility of achieving their aspirations slipping away. We are not the people that we want to be and are capable of becoming, and the great advances in knowledge, industry and material well-being that have marked this century have brought us no closer to realizing our potential.

Many Americans think that religion can bring us closer to realizing this potential. Religion defines one's relationship with someone or something greater than herself, and thus helps her to create a vision or a dream of what she might become. Perhaps, then, Americans can hope to be a better nation and people than they are now. To the extent that religion fills the existing spiritual void with the hope and the reality of building better lives, it will continue to grow in influence at every level of contemporary American life.

Religion is a matter of community and national importance, and not merely a personal matter whose significance is confined to those who believe. Religion has a powerful public dimension as well as a private one. What one believes to be ultimately right and true affects every aspect of her life—who she votes for, what laws are desirable, how to teach her children, how to describe and judge the world in which she lives and the people with whom she interacts. Yet the presumption of cultural elites at least since World War II has been that religion has no public role to play in any of these matters. Since religious beliefs are thought to matter only for those who believe, such beliefs are out of place in any venue where nonbelievers are present. The constitutional division of church and state in the United States, for example, generally has been interpreted during the last 40 years to exclude all meaningful manifestations of religion from the institutions and processes of public life.

A political conflict from the 1970s illustrates how deeply the separation ethic has penetrated American public life. After the Supreme Court ruled in 1973 that women have a constitutional right to abortion in most circumstances,[1] one prolife tactic focused on halting public funding of abortions performed under the auspices of government welfare programs. This movement achieved considerable successes, among them the passage of the Hyde Amendment, which denied federal funding for all abortions except those performed to save the life of the mother. Noting that the prolife movement was dominated by Catholics, fundamentalist Protestants, Mormons, orthodox Jews, and others acting on prolife religious beliefs, prochoice activists challenged the Hyde Amendment as an unconstitutional establishment of religion.[2] Although this argument ultimately was rejected by the Supreme Court, it was taken seriously by the legal system, and at one time garnered considerable support in the legal community.[3]

Many religious people in the United States would have been surprised to learn that their mere support of legislative initiatives was construed by some to violate the Constitution. However, to a legal community operating on the assumption that "religious belief and practice are fanatical and superstitious[,] the opposing enemy of reason and the good society,"[4] the argument was plausible, if not obvious. To them, the prolife movement was motivated by the goal of imposing antiabortion theology on everyone through generally applicable legislation like the Hyde Amendment. It is noteworthy that no parallel constitutional challenge was undertaken to the liberal ideology that underlies the prochoice movement, even though that ideology would itself have been imposed upon the country had the Hyde Amendment been rejected. This parallel challenge, however, would not have been taken seriously by lawyers and judges. Religion is out of place in the secularism of public life; "secular humanism," on the other hand, is by definition quite at home there.

Even though the argument against the Hyde Amendment was ultimately rejected, the fact that it could have been made at all and receive serious attention and support suggests an assumption about the interaction of religion with the institutions and processes of American public life: religion does not belong in public. This banishment of religion from public life creates in religious Americans a strong sense of frustration. Their most important and sacred beliefs are deemed inappropriate or unimportant by the cultural elites who influence the agenda of public life. Participation in public life too often forces one to reject or to disguise religious beliefs in favor of more worldly, temporal, and nonreligious ways of thinking. The price of acceptance in public life is discarding one's personal religious identity. Religious Americans are thus separated and excluded—"alienated"—from public life.

The American stage has been set for a series of collisions between religious individuals and institutions and the practitioners of elite culture who represent the government and the other institutions which influence the content of American public life. These custodians of public life generally do not wish any greater public manifestations of religious sentiment than are already present in American society. In fact, the status quo may already permit more public religion than many of them would like. They would keep religion and religious belief scrupulously private.

Religious people see this as conscious discrimination against them and their religious beliefs, discrimination so sweeping and thorough that they look in vain for the sacred in their schools, in popular entertainment, or in literature, drama, politics, or law. There is a disquieting similarity between government treatment of religious institutions and individuals in the United States and their treatment in aggressively and pervasively secular states. Although in the United States one is free in theory to participate in public life as a religious person, in practice public life does not value religion. In the United States, one clearly is free to believe, to speak, and to act religiously in one's personal, private life. It remains a point of conflict and controversy, however, whether such expressions are proper in a public setting.

The most recent turn to religion, then, will inevitably spawn a crisis in American government and politics. The outlines of that crisis are already visible in the controversial reentry of fundamentalist Protestants into American politics during the 1970s. Religious Americans are unwilling either to discard their personal religiosity or to divorce it from their public lives. Their churches and other religious associations likewise are unwilling to steer their ministries clear of matters of public concern. Both religious individuals and religious institutions are demanding that their beliefs be taken seriously. They are vigorously challenging the secularist assumption that religion is inherently irrational, subjective, and violent. They seek cooperation from government, not hostility and separation. Each time the custodians of public life rebuff incursions of religion into the public arena, religious Americans become more frustrated, angrier and more strident in their insistence that religion be included in public life.

These are critical times. If religion is not accepted into American public life, then ultimately religious Americans could become so frustrated in their assaults upon the secularism of public life that they would threaten the viability of the current social order—they might revolt. We think this unlikely because of the pragmatic nature of American democracy. Historically, radical movements in the United States have not succeeded in overthrowing the system, because the system eventually accedes to the most popular and powerful of their demands. Once a radical movement grows to the point that it becomes a genuine threat to existing bases of political power, mainstream politicians tend to adopt elements of the radical program as their own so as to preempt its urgency and appeal. The 1960s and 1970s saw the growth of African American revolutionaries in the United States in response to the slow and halting recognition of civil rights for people of color. Once these movements became a potent political and social force, however, federal and state governments themselves incorporated minority civil rights into their agenda. In similar fashion, the American socialist movement of the 1920s was coopted by the dramatic expansion of social welfare programs during the New Deal era.

We believe that the same process of acceptance and accommodation will occur with respect to contemporary assertions of religion in public life. American government will preempt the radicalization and revolution of alienated religious Americans by partially incorporating and otherwise adjusting to their religious concerns. (This process may already have started with the Republican Party's concessions to the religious right.) Thus, we applaud the turn to religion (although not necessarily the religious right) because, in the end, we believe that the United States will emerge from this confrontation between secularists and sectarians better equipped to accommodate and respond to the spiritual needs and diversity of its people. By admitting religion into the mainstream of its public life, the United States can become a more vital, democratic, and culturally honest society. Why and how this is coming to pass is the subject of this book.

At a time when religion is again the subject of intense public scrutiny, it is important to clarify what we mean by "religion." Philosopher Bertrand Russell described the great historical religions as complex social phenomena that have typically entailed an institutional structure, a theological creed, and a personal moral code.[5] Sociologist Clifford Geertz defined religion as an activity that involves an ultimate concern, a social structure and behavioral code, rites and ceremonies, symbolic or mythic language and narrative, and the belief in something metaphysical or transcendent which goes beyond what one can observe with the senses.[6]

Certainly the sweep of religion is far broader than the rantings of erstwhile televangelists who commit the very sins they electronically condemn. It is broader, too, than the Christian right which sees room in America for no religion but its own, and the Christian left which has become, in Richard Neuhaus's phrase, a "wholly owned subsidiary of the Democratic party." For us, American religion includes the traditional religions of the West—Judaism, Catholicism, Islam, and Protestantism—as well as those indigenous to the United States itself—Mormonism, Adventism, Christian Science, and the Jehovah's Witnesses. Increasingly, especially on the Pacific coast, it also includes the religions of the East—Buddhism, Hinduism, and the "New Wave" religions they have inspired. American religion has always included the novel and the bizarre, the criminal and the fraudulent, although in fact these have manifested themselves in our religious history much less often than conventional secular wisdom has assumed.

Although no one of these fully captures the reality of religion in America, all of them at some level share at least one theme which both Russell and Geertz touch on as well: God—whether from within or from without—talks to humanity, the transcendent condescending to the mundane. Indeed, the remarkable aspect of the recurring religious imbroglios of televangelists and others is not that so many self-righteous ministers sin, but rather that their congregations forgive them. These congregations may be naive and stupid, duped by the new Elmer Gantrys of contemporary life. They may also be longing for the spiritual knowledge of religious experience so badly that they accept the hypocrisy of its exponents as the price of spiritual fulfillment. This longing for transcendent and enduring meaning is the "religion" that we assume, and about which we write.

## NOTES

1. Roe v. Wade, 410 U.S. 113 (1973).
2. McRae v. Califano, 491 F. Supp. 630, 690–723 (E.D.N.Y. 1979), *rev'd sub. nom.* Harris v. McRae, 448 U.S. 297 (1980).
3. E.g., Laurence Tribe, "Foreword: Toward a Model of Roles in the Due Process of Life and Law," *Harvard Law Review* 87 (1973): 1; Note, "Rebuilding the Wall: The Case for a Return to the Strict Interpretation of the Establishment Clause," *Columbia Law Review* 81 (1981): 1463 (student author); Note, "Abortion, Medicaid, and the Constitution," *New York University Law Review* 54 (1980): 120, 151–55 (student author).
4. Ruel W. Tyson, Jr., "Introduction" to *The Religion Beat: The Reporting of Religion in the Media.* Conference Report (New York: The Rockefeller Foundation, 1981), 1, 4.
5. Bertrand Russell, *Religion and Science* (New York: Oxford University Press, 1961), 8.
6. Clifford Geertz, *The Interpretation of Cultures: Selected Essays* (New York: Basic, 1973), 90–91.

# Part I

## Religion in America

*Chapter 1*

# The Paradox of Religion in America

Perhaps no aspect of life in the United States is more celebrated than the religious vitality of American society. Yet national pride in this attribute disguises a paradox about religion in the United States: Although in their personal lives Americans have remained actively religious throughout the 20th century, little evidence of this religious commitment leaks into the contemporary public sphere of American life. One observer of the American cultural scene has noted that "no other Western nation has such a high proportion of citizens who believe and practice a religion—and yet it often seems that virtually all serious analysis of the culture is conducted by the remainder of the population."[1] Despite the United States' status as perhaps the most religiously plural of contemporary democracies, one searches in vain for religion in politics, law, government, media, or the arts. This public triumph of "secularism"—that way of thinking and living which rejects, excludes, or ignores religious experience and belief—has alienated millions of religious people from American public life, and thus is at the heart of the cultural and political crisis caused by the recent turn to religion.

## RELIGION IN AMERICAN PRIVATE LIFE

There has been great variety in the religious beliefs of Americans from the earliest political origins of the United States.[2] Even colonial America was composed of a diversity of Protestant sects, as well as Roman Catholics and Jews. As a matter of practicality and pragmatism, the diversity of religions in the United States has forced Americans to learn to get along despite their religious differences in order for society to function. This is not to say that relations have been perfect; on the contrary, religious persecution and even bloodshed have been part of American history, and to some extent remain even in this supposedly enlightened age. Nevertheless, Americans are unusually tolerant about religion in comparison to the attitudes of people living in other Western countries. Perhaps as a result, the United States has been fertile soil for new religions as well as more established ones, and religious groups have typically participated in most aspects of private life in the United States. There are now over 200 distinct religious denominations in the United States, with their adherents organized into nearly 350,000 separate churches and other religious congregations and groups.[3]

By describing people or organizations as "religious," we mean that religion occupies a central role in ordering their priorities and choices in life. More than one-quarter of all inhabitants of the United States, and perhaps as many as one-half, are religious in this sense. Empirical studies consistently demonstrate the deep commitment of contemporary Americans to traditional religious beliefs, practices, and institutions. This commitment is evident whether the data are subjectively or objectively generated—that is, whether one measures what people *say* they think about religion, or rather measures activities that show what people actually *do* about religion.

For example, recent polls have reported that 91 percent of Americans state a religious preference, 71 percent claim membership in a church or synagogue, 58 percent to 61 percent believe that religion can solve all or most of today's problems, 57 percent have high levels of confidence in organized religion, 55 percent to 56 percent state that religion is very important and 31 percent that religion is fairly important in their lives, and 40 percent to 42 percent attend a church or synagogue during a typical week.[4] An exhaustive study of American values conducted in 1980 found that 74 percent of Americans consider themselves religious, and 49 percent can identify a specific time in their adult lives when they made "a personal commitment to Christ" which changed their lives.

It also found that 73 percent of Americans frequently feel that God loves them, 57 percent frequently engage in prayer, 44 percent frequently attend religious services, 28 percent frequently read the Bible, 25 percent frequently participate in church socials, 23 percent frequently encourage others to be religious, 21 percent frequently listen to religious broadcasts, and 26 percent frequently engage in or experience at least five of these activities and feelings.[5]

An in-depth sociological study of religious belief and practice in a Midwestern city from 1924 to 1978 found that among married couples, rates of activity and membership in churches are higher than those of any other social organization, and that charitable contributions to churches were more than four times those to secular charities.[6] A recent survey of average weekly church attendance conducted in 24 countries worldwide found the United States at 43 percent trailing only Malta (91 percent), Ireland (72 percent), Mexico (54 percent), Northern Ireland (52 percent), and white South Africa (50 percent).[7]

Although subject to some year-to-year fluctuation, the empirical data on the religiosity of Americans have been generally stable since the 1920s. Pollster George Gallup writes that "the most appropriate word to use to describe the religious character of the nation as a whole over the last half century is 'stability.' Basic religious beliefs, and even religious practice, differ relatively little from the levels recorded 50 years ago. In fact, the nation has in some respects remained remarkably orthodox— even fundamentalist—in its beliefs."[8] Indeed, with one exception, the American people currently appear to be as religious as they have been at any time since the 19th century. The exception would be the 1950s, when American religious devotion reached its high-water mark of this century.

## SECULARISM IN AMERICAN PUBLIC LIFE

The continuing and pervasive influence of religion in the personal lives of Americans stands in stark contrast to the influence of religion in American public life. By "public life," we mean those spheres and aspects of American life in which large numbers of Americans communicate and interact on a regional or national scale. Certainly an experience or relationship has a significant public aspect to it if it is shared or duplicated across the country. Public life in the United States thus would include national and state politics, federal and state legal systems, and the collection and distribution of news and information through national newspapers and magazines.

In addition, the national broadcast of television news and entertainment programming forms part of American public life, and may well eclipse the role of the print media. Although public schools in the United States have traditionally been subject to local control, the vastly increased federal and state control of public education and the continued interaction of the great majority of Americans with public education suggest that it also should be considered a component of American public life. Higher

education in both state-sponsored and private universities and foundations supports a national community of scholars, artists, and other
intellectuals, and exerts an influence on American public life dispropor-
tionate to its numbers.

All of these institutions and processes operate on the assumption that
a secularized public life is both necessary and desirable. Among those
who function in the world of American public life, writes Richard
Neuhaus, a frequent commentator on religion in the United States,

> the idea is widely accepted that religion is something between an
> individual and his God. Each person is free to worship the god of
> her choice. Religion is the business of church and home and has no
> place in public space . . . . Legally and politically, [this axiom is]
> supported by a notion of the "separation of church and state" that
> is understood to mean the separation of religion and religiously
> based morality from the public realm.[9]

The different arenas of public life reflect little evidence of the
profoundly religious character of large numbers of Americans. The
judiciary long ago expelled religion from the public schools. Most
Americans are aware that the Supreme Court has found public school
prayer to be unconstitutional. The Court also has invalidated on-campus
religious instruction, classroom display of the Ten Commandments,
so-called "moments of silence" at the beginning of the school day that
encourage individual prayer, and the teaching of creationist theories
about the earth's origin which suggest the possibility of divine participation.[10] Before the Supreme Court (cautiously) approved religiously
oriented student clubs in public high schools, numerous lower courts had
prohibited them from organizing and functioning at public schools, even
when student participation was genuinely voluntary and the religious
clubs satisfied the same requirements that were imposed on secular
clubs.[11]

The secularism of the public schools, however, is not solely the result
of intervention by the courts. Textbooks chosen by public schools in
conjunction with their curriculum have generally ignored religion. Dr.
Paul Vitz of New York University has conducted an extensive survey of
public school texts documenting their general secular bias. He found that
religion in public school textbooks tends to be presented primarily in
contexts that are chronologically or culturally distant from contemporary
American life, with little or no discussion of current religious movements
and traditions in the United States. For example, textbooks will discuss

subjects like the development of Buddhist thought in the ancient Far East, but rarely refer to the revitalization of Catholicism in the United States and elsewhere since the Second Vatican Council. Similarly, some textbooks appear to have censored material relating to the most common religious preferences of Americans while including material about less common religions. One book, for example, devotes substantial space to Muhammad and the rise of Islam while giving little or no attention to Jesus and Christianity. The texts also tend to ignore the Protestant Reformation, the founding and development of Mormonism, Adventism, Christian Science, and other distinctly American religions, the influence of conservative Protestantism in American history, and the positive contributions of Catholicism and Judaism to American social reform.

Perhaps most disturbing, Vitz found numerous texts in which the religious dimension of historical events is simply deleted, such as descriptions of colonial American pilgrims as "people who make long trips" without reference to their religious motives and character, and discussions of Joan of Arc that do not mention God, revelation, Catholicism, or sainthood.[12] In sum, Vitz found that insofar as public school textbooks discuss religion at all, they treat only religions that are chronologically, culturally, or geographically remote from contemporary American life.

Other studies have generated similar results. Summarizing this state of affairs, a report of the Association for Supervision and Curriculum Development states that "references to religion have been all but excised from the public school curriculum."[13] The report indicates that even college-level courses "have for decades neglected to focus on historical or contemporary expression of religion in American and world cultures or on the influence of religious texts in world literature."[14]

The secularism in American public schools enforced by the Supreme Court and reinforced by textbooks has by now been internalized by teachers and administrators. The de facto policy of the majority of public school boards in the United States has been to eliminate all hints of religious material from the curriculum. In part, this has been the result of the understandable perception that the Supreme Court has prohibited references to religion in public schools. Also playing a part have been the parochial concerns of religious parents, who often want *their* religious views taught in public schools, but nobody else's.

One might argue that many administrators simply have found ignoring religion to be the path of least controversy. However, many subjects of the public school curriculum, like evolution and sex education, have generated parental opposition in the past, yet school boards, administrators, and teachers have not hesitated to insist in the face of controversy that these subjects are essential to a well-rounded education. Thus, eliminating religion from the public school curriculum may also reflect, in addition to conflict-avoidance on the part of administrators, the widespread assumption of professional educators that "religion is 'the dead hand of the past,' at best unimportant in modern life and at worst destructive."[15]

Consider, for example, lower court litigation under the Equal Access Act. The Act was passed by Congress in 1987 to ensure that student religious organizations like Bible study groups would be granted the same access to public high school facilities as secular student clubs. As we indicated, the Act was recently upheld by the Supreme Court. The Act does not apply, however, unless the high school maintains a "public forum," which occurs whenever a high school grants access to groups or clubs that are not related to the school's curriculum. In virtually every Equal Access case, one finds public school administrators taking the position that their school has not created a public forum, in a transparent attempt to deny access to religious groups under the Act. They testify that chess clubs are related to mathematics, logic, and critical thinking; that bowling and scuba-diving clubs are related to physical fitness; and that service clubs are related to sociology and psychology.[16]

Of course, at this level of generality and abstraction, religious groups can make equally plausible claims of curriculum relatedness through their obvious relevance to history, literature, sociology, and current events. Even prayer and Bible-reading encourage a pious personal responsibility on the part of students, and thus have a clear connection to the social obligations and psychological health of students in an era of teen pregnancy and substance abuse. To the extent that the claim of curriculum relatedness is unpersuasive as to religious groups, it should likewise be unpersuasive regarding the secular groups. By making these weak claims of curriculum relatedness for secular groups but not religious ones, administrators reveal their preference for keeping religion off the public school campus.

Failing to teach about the historical and social importance of religion in the United States and elsewhere is a failure of public education. It implicitly denies the relevance of religion to contemporary life and ignores its importance to the formation of the American nation and the historical development of its culture and politics. The educational establishment in the United States is slowly coming to recognize this. Nevertheless, secularists continue to describe public education as "a most powerful ally" and "the most important factor moving us toward a secular society."[17] Certainly if public education were the only measure of past and present American religiosity, one would have to conclude not only that God and his followers are dead, but that they never even existed.

Popular culture as well as public education generally ignores religion. Until very recently, one rarely saw a normal television family that attends services, even if only on Christmas and Easter, or Rosh Hashanah or Yom Kippur. This is despite the fact that nearly half of all Americans attend services at a church or synagogue at least once a month. Such depictions of religious devotion passed from the cultural scene more than a generation ago. Contemporary religious television characters tend to be either comedic caricatures or corrupted hypocrites. Religious devotion is presented more often as the object of humor or even ridicule than as a normal part of the life of nearly half the country.

Even when television portrays the life of a real person, it often deemphasizes or altogether ignores the individual's religious beliefs. Several years ago CBS broadcast a movie, *Nobody's Child*, about the life of a woman who had gained release from a state mental institution after the ordeal of 20 years of confinement. In actual life, the woman is a deeply religious person who credits her faith in God with sustaining her throughout her long confinement. The movie, however, did not depict this dimension of her life in any way.

Similarly, the news media rarely acknowledge the existence and significance of the religious beliefs held by those they report on, except to expose and emphasize hypocrisy. For example, contrary to popular belief, American politicians seem to be as broadly and deeply influenced by religion as other Americans. One study conducted by political scientists Peter Benson and Dorothy Williams of the University of Minnesota found that members of Congress are as religious as the rest of the American public, and in some ways even more religious. Benson and Williams believe that the widespread perception to the contrary is due in part to the failure of the national news media to include religion in their reporting on Capitol Hill.

Noting that the overwhelming majority of reporters for the most respected and prominent of the media are not religious, they suggest that these reporters are either uninterested in or unable to recognize religious influences in Congress. Thus, consciously or unconsciously, these reporters filter religion from congressional news and contribute to the erroneous impression that "religion is not an important part of life for members of Congress."[18] Richard Neuhaus witnessed a related phenomenon firsthand as an aide to Dr. Martin Luther King, Jr. during the civil rights era, reporting that the television cameras were always turned off

when Dr. King began to speak of the religious justifications for racial
equality.[19]

Literary critic Mark Edmundson has pointed out that many of the most
influential contemporary journalists were educated in the 1960s by
English professors at elite universities who believed that literature had
replaced religion as the principal source of moral values.[20] Even so-called
"religion reporters," who specialize in reporting on religious issues and
events, are usually nonbelievers.[21] It stands to reason, then, that journalists might view religion as a public influence of declining importance,
if they see it as a significant public influence at all. There is widespread
belief among the religious and nonreligious alike that Americans are
becoming ever more secular in their approach to modern life. Curiously,
there is little empirical support for this notion, as we have discussed.
However well it may describe American public life, "secular" is grossly
inaccurate when applied to the private lives of a large number of
Americans.

The exclusion of religion from politics and government is somewhat
more complicated, though no less real. The activism of religious groups
in contemporary politics is obvious on both the left and the right of the
political spectrum. From the liberal National Council of Churches to the
conservative fundamentalist Protestants of the so-called "religious
right," religious groups have been active and successful in influencing
political campaigns and government legislation and regulations. In light
of this, describing religion as having been "excluded" from politics and
government, as we do, seems inaccurate.

Accordingly, we emphasize that religious groups and individuals can
successfully participate in contemporary American politics only if they
participate as *interest* groups, rather than *religious* groups. Any person
or entity who convincingly demonstrates an ability to deliver large
numbers of votes in an election will be listened to by political representatives. Churches and other religious groups have enjoyed considerable
success in pursuit of their agenda through contemporary interest group
politics. In this respect, however, they differ little from the hundreds of
organizations which seek to shape state and federal legislation in ways
that will benefit themselves. A religion in this mode expresses itself
merely as a self-interested preference, like Wall Street investment
bankers who support a capital gains tax cut, or labor unions that oppose
right-to-work laws.

By contrast, a religion enters political dialogue as religion, and not
merely as an interest group, when it seeks to provide a distinctive point
of moral reference to public policy debates. This has been the traditional

voice of religions in American politics, and a very powerful one. One thinks here of the anti-slavery activism of northern Protestant abolitionists in the pre–Civil War era; the fundamentalists of the temperance and suffrage movements during the early 20th century; the early civil rights activism of liberal Protestants, Catholics, and Jews; and the antiabortion stance of the Roman Catholic Church and other religious groups in contemporary politics.

These religious individuals and groups did not enter these debates to protect an economic or other such interest, in the way that secular lobbying groups normally do; rather, they sought to witness against moral wrongs by testifying of transcendent truth. The abolitionists entered the national debate on slavery because they believed the practice violated divine truths about human dignity and freedom. The fundamentalists sought to reverse dehumanizing social trends which they attributed to unregulated capitalism and modernization at the turn of the 19th century. Religious activists of the civil rights era worked to eradicate the evil and oppression of American apartheid. The Catholic hierarchy today believes that abortion violates transcendent truths about the sanctity of unborn life. These individuals and groups did not become politically involved because they believed the disputed practices undermined one of their "interests." Indeed, if that had been their dominant motivation, it is doubtful that they could have spoken with such moral power and persuasion.

However successful churches and other religious groups may be in gaining political and legislative recognition of their parochial concerns in contemporary politics, their attempts to enter political dialogue as distinctive moral voices generally have not been welcomed. There remains considerable controversy about whether religion should play any distinctive role in American public life.

The last 20 years have seen a resurgence of political and social activism by religious groups at all points of the political spectrum. Yet this rediscovered activism has called forth strident, emotional attacks on religion by those who see public religion on the left or the right as an unacceptable threat to constitutional liberties and conventional politics. Public religious activity causes near-hysteria on the part of people at both ends of the political spectrum. Consider the inflammatory titles of some publications during the last decade—*Holy Terror: The Fundamentalist War on America's Freedoms in Religion, Politics, and Our Private Lives*,[22] and *The Church and the Sword: How the Churches and Peace Movement Are Disarming America—and What You Can Do About It*.[23]

Similarly, recent court decisions that have constitutionally validated certain public religious activities[24] have been widely and vehemently condemned by legal academics as striking at the very foundations of American constitutional principles. Secular political activists persist in bringing litigation—like the lawsuit seeking to force revocation of the tax-exempt status of the Roman Catholic Church in the United States[25]— with the aim of penalizing or crippling churches that dare to speak with a moral voice on political issues. Religion is welcomed in political life only if it abandons its spiritual soul.

It can be argued that the twin assumptions of religious privatization and public secularization emanate only from a relatively small number of social groups, such as public educators, judges, intellectuals, artists, media representatives, and the like. Even combined, these groups are numerically insignificant compared to the rest of the United States. However, social power and influence are not always proportionate to numbers. All of these groups exert considerable cultural influence in the United States. In public education and television, for example, one has the two institutions that occupy most of the waking hours of American children. All of the institutions and processes of American public life are disproportionately influential in the formation, shaping, and maintenance of American public opinion. They contribute mightily to the cultural backdrop that informs the individual attitudes and decisions of each citizen. Since these groups act on the assumption that religion should be excluded from public life, one should not be surprised to see that assumption replicated in various ways throughout American society, despite the persistent private beliefs of religious Americans.

We emphasize that we do not believe in some grand conspiracy of "godless humanists" aimed at stamping out religion. Rather, various influences have combined in subtle, unconnected, and largely unconscious ways to create a "cultural presumption" of secularism in public life. Certainly the modern affinity for science and individualism does not easily mesh with religion, which so often entails unprovable faith and devotion to community. Thus, almost without thinking, modern participants in the public arena assume that religion is a private phenomenon that is irrelevant, inappropriate, and even dangerous in public. Despite the fact that Americans remain profoundly committed to religion in private, American public culture barely reflects any meaningful religious content.

# NOTES

1. Peter Steinfels, "Public News, Private Religion" in *The Religion Beat: The Reporting of Religion in the Media.* Conference Report (New York: The Rockefeller Foundation, 1981), 27, 30–31.

2. Thomas Curry, *The First Freedoms: Church and State in America to the Passage of the First Amendment* (New York: Oxford University Press, 1986), chaps. 1–3; A. James Reichley, *Religion in American Public Life* (Washington, D.C.: Brookings, 1985), 170–77.

3. Constant A. Jacquet, Jr., ed., *Yearbook of American and Canadian Churches 1987* (Nashville, Tenn.: Abingdon, 1987); Frank S. Mead, *Handbook of Denominations in the United States,* 6th ed. (Nashville, Tenn.: Abingdon, 1975). See also Theodore Caplow, Howard Bahr, and Bruce Chadwick, *All Faithful People: Change and Continuity in Middletown's Religion* (Minneapolis: University of Minnesota Press, 1983), 310; Reichley, *Religion in America,* 8.

4. George Gallup, Jr., *The Gallup Poll: Public Opinion 1986* (Wilmington, Del.: Scholarly Resources, 1987), 6, 9, 10, 15, 127, 272–73, 280; George Gallup, Jr., *The Gallup Poll: Public Opinion 1985* (Wilmington, Del.: Scholarly Resources, 1986), 120–21, 162, 291.

5. *The Connecticut Mutual Life Report on American Values in the '80's: The Impact of Belief* (New York: Research Forecasts, 1981), 41–43.

6. Caplow, et. al., *All Faithful People,* 84–86, 309.

7. Jacquet, *1987 Yearbook,* 286.

8. George Gallup, Jr., "50 Years of Gallup Surveys on Religion," *The Gallup Report* (May 1985): 5.

9. Richard John Neuhaus, *The Naked Public Square: Religion and Democracy in America,* 2d ed. (Grand Rapids, Mich.: Eerdmans, 1986), 20.

10. E.g., Edwards v. Aguillard, 482 U.S. 578 (1987) (invalidating teaching of creationism); Wallace v. Jaffree, 472 U.S. 38 (1985) (invalidating religiously motivated moments of silence); Stone v. Graham, 449 U.S. 39 (1980) (invalidating display of Ten Commandments); Epperson v. Arkansas, 393 U.S. 97 (1968) (invalidating prohibition on teaching evolution); Abington School District v. Schempp, 374 U.S. 203 (1963) (invalidating prayer and Bible reading); Engel v. Vitale, 370 U.S. 421 (1962) (invalidating prayer); McCollum v. Board of Education, 333 U.S. 203 (1948) (invalidating on-campus religious instruction).

11. E.g., Bender v. Williamsport Area School District, 741 F.2d 538 (3d Cir. 1984), *vacated on other grounds,* 475 U.S. 534 (1986) (lack of standing to bring appeal); Garnett v. Renton School District No. 403, 874 F.2d 608 (9th Cir. 1989); Nartowicz v. Clayton City School District, 736 F.2d 646 (11th Cir. 1984); Lubbock Civil Liberties Union v. Lubbock Independent School District, 669 F.2d 1038 (5th Cir.), *cert. denied,* 459 U.S. 1155 (1983); Brandon v. Board of Education, 635 F.2d 971 (2d Cir. 1980), *cert. denied,* 454 U.S. 1123 (1981). In Board of Education v. Mergens, 110 S.Ct. 2356 (1990), the Supreme Court upheld the practice of granting religiously oriented student clubs access to high school campus facilities, although no single opinion was joined by a majority of the justices.

12. Paul Vitz, *Religion and Traditional Values in Public School Textbooks: An Empirical Study* (Washington, D.C.: National Institute of Education, 1985), 21–25, 32–36, 41–44, 65, 70.

13. *Religion in the Curriculum: A Report from the ASCD Panel on Religion in the Curriculum* (Alexandria, Va.: Association for Supervision and Curriculum Development, 1987), 7.

14. Ibid., 11.

15. Ibid., 16.

16. E.g., Mergens v. Board of Education, 867 F.2d 1076, 1078 (8th Cir. 1988), *aff'd*, 110 S.Ct. 2356 (1990); Garnett v. Renton School District No. 403, 675 F. Supp. 1268, 1273 (W.D. Wash. 1987), *aff'd*, 874 F.2d 608 (9th Cir. 1989).

17. Quoted in James Kilpatrick, "Public Schools Face a Thorny Religion Issue," *Macon Telegraph & News*, February 18, 1986.

18. Peter Benson and Dorothy Williams, *Religion on Capitol Hill: Myths and Realities* (New York: Oxford University Press, 1986), 72–84.

19. Neuhaus, *Naked Public Square*, 98.

20. Mark Edmundson, "A Will to Cultural Power: Deconstructing the DeMan Scandal," *Harper's Magazine* 227 (July 1988): 67, 69–70. See also Terry Eagleton, *Literary Theory: An Introduction* (Minneapolis: University of Minnesota Press, 1983), 22–23, 93.

21. John Dart, "The Religion Beat," in *The Religion Beat*, 19, 20–21.

22. Flo Conway and Joel Siegleman, *Holy Terror: The Fundamentalist Lives* (New York: Dell, 1982).

23. G. Russell Evans and C. Gregg Singer, *The Church and the Sword: How the Churches and Peace Movement Are Disarming America—and What You Can Do About It*, rev. 2d ed. (Fletcher, N.C.: New Puritan, 1983).

24. E.g., Lynch v. Donnelly, 465 U.S. 668 (1984) (municipal display of crèche); Marsh v. Chambers, 463 U.S. 783 (1983) (legislative prayer).

25. Abortion Rights Mobilization, Inc. v. Baker, 110 F.R.D. 337 (S.D.N.Y. 1986), *aff'd sub nom.* In re United States Catholic Conference, 824 F.2d 156 (2d Cir. 1987), *rev'd sub nom.* United States Catholic Conference v. Abortion Rights Mobilization, Inc., 108 S.Ct. 2268 (1988); Abortion Rights Mobilization, Inc. v. Baker, 603 F. Supp. 970 (S.D.N.Y. 1985), *aff'd*, 788 F.2d 3 (2d Cir.), *cert. denied*, 479 U.S. (1986); 552 F. Supp. 364 (S.D.N.Y. 1982); 544 F. Supp. 471 (S.D.N.Y. 1982). See also McRae v. Califano, 491 F. Supp. 630 (E.D.N.Y. 1979), *rev'd sub nom.* Harris v. McRae, 448 U.S. 297 (1980).

*Chapter 2*

# The Threat of Religion in America

The paradox of religion in America is that American public life has become overwhelmingly secular at the same time that large numbers of Americans have remained strongly committed to traditional religious beliefs and activities. One consequence of this state of affairs is that many religious Americans feel estranged from the institutions and processes of American public life. Any society, even one based on a tolerant and well-functioning democracy, can expect to have some portion of its citizenry disaffected with the status quo at any given time. When large numbers of citizens feel distanced from the institutions and processes that constitute the society in which they live, however, the seeds of revolution have been sown. Americans are used to thinking of revolution as something that happens in distant third world countries, not in the United States. Although we agree that religious revolution in the United States is unlikely, the potential for it is nonetheless present. More important, the consequences of religious alienation are serious and significant even if, as one might expect, they fall short of revolt.

## PUBLIC IMPLICATIONS OF PRIVATE RELIGIOUS VALUES

Many would argue that the absence of religion from public life is desirable. Religious participation in politics and other public policy debates is frequently criticized because it polarizes the political community on issues that do not lend themselves to the essential political processes of fact-finding and compromise. In a Supreme Court opinion from the 1970s, Justice John Harlan argued that the involvement of religion in politics is a constitutional evil even when it does not infringe upon the religious liberty of individuals and organizations. Such involvement, he argued,

> is apt to lead to strife and frequently strain a political system to the breaking point . . . . Religious groups inevitably represent certain points of view and not infrequently assert them in the political arena, as evidenced by the continuing debate respecting birth control and abortion laws. Yet history cautions that political fragmentation on sectarian lines must be guarded against.[1]

The key to avoidance of this religious fragmentation, Harlan thought, was general exclusion of religion from politics. If religion is completely disabled from participating in the political process, then it will not be able to exert its fractious and fragmenting influence on political issues, or so the argument goes. Presumably the political process generates enough division and controversy on its own without the moral absolutism of religious belief.

This same kind of argument has been directed lately by the political left against the current political activism of the resurgent religious right. Politically active religious fundamentalists are accused of advocating religious oppression, because of their substantive agenda, as well as the manner in which that agenda is pursued. The religious right tends not to soften its arguments and positions upon entering the political arena. This unwillingness to dilute or to compromise its religious morality is seen as evidence that the religious right is pursuing a vision of America in which Jews, Muslims, atheists, and other non-Christians do not appear. Ironically, 25 years ago it was the political right which criticized the participation of the religious left in the civil rights, antiwar, and antipoverty movements. In both cases, the objection was that religious experience and its accompanying morality are matters of personal piety and unyielding conviction; bringing one's religious beliefs into the public arena as the basis for government action, therefore, is thought highly inappropriate, a public imposition of private and personal beliefs.

This view of religion has important implications for the political process in the United States. It presupposes that religious and moral principles are wholly subjective—that is, completely irrelevant in judging the behavior and actions of other people. This subjectivity is thought to render religious and moral principles out of place in politics. Since a religious belief, such as a belief that a fetus is a fully human life, is binding only on those who belong to the religious community that holds the belief, legislating or regulating the entire population on the basis of the belief is an unfair imposition of one's religious morality on others. Accordingly, those who are prochoice on the abortion question accuse their opponents of trying to force their prolife religious beliefs on the entire country. Why, they ask, cannot prolifers be content with renouncing abortion themselves, while letting others who disagree make their own decisions about the morality of choosing abortion?

One answer is obvious. Some values are not considered to be incontrovertible matters of individual taste and preference to be decided by each person on her own. The subjective view of values—that resolving conflicts in values is rightfully left to the individual—is acceptable only if one is more or less indifferent to how that choice might be exercised by others. Decisions not to use tobacco products or to consume alcoholic beverages are this kind of value decision. So long as the harmful effects of such activities on others—secondhand smoke and drunken driving— are minimized, the general feeling even among those who choose not to smoke or drink is that such activities need not be prohibited outright.

Some values may reflect upon such critical matters, however, and may be held and believed so strongly, that those who hold them do not view them as being subject to compromise. If one sincerely believes that abortion is murder, for example, then simply to avoid committing it oneself does not satisfy the imperative for moral action; clearly, no one should be permitted to commit murder. Thus, one who holds this view of abortion will feel compelled to demonstrate support for laws and other government action that would make it difficult for anyone else to commit what she believes to be a most grievous moral wrong. Indeed, such a person might even feel compelled to violate existing law in service to the greater moral good of preventing abortion.

Many prolife activists feel exactly this way. They style themselves as championing the cause of a vulnerable and persecuted minority, like the abolitionists who fought against slavery more than a century ago. "Choice," in this context, is rather beside the point, since it compromises a value—the sanctity of unborn life—that simply is not "up for grabs."

There is also a deeper sense in which moral values, including religious beliefs, can never be wholly subjective. By this we mean that the consequences of making a moral choice are rarely confined to the chooser. What a society permits its members to do sends unmistakable messages about what that society considers to be right behavior, and what it considers to be wrong behavior.

In a very real sense, the moral choices of any person in a society affect the moral choices of everybody else in that society. Moral thinking in general provides behavioral norms, standards, and values that guide one's everyday living. In the United States, moral thinking includes religious as well as nonreligious value systems. The religious and nonreligious norms, standards, and values held by the political majority are quite naturally reflected in the laws and regulations generated by a democratic government. Indeed, the laws and regulations by which a people choose to govern themselves tell that people something about who they are.

In the United States, as in other countries, our laws contribute to a sense of both national and personal identity. For example, the Constitution of the United States and its Amendments—particularly the first 10 Amendments which constitute the Bill of Rights—are a central influence in the self-understanding of those who live under its authority. That is, these texts strongly affect how Americans live and think of themselves as Americans. In part because the founding political document of the United States is thought to protect the liberty and equality of all Americans, we consider ourselves to be a people that loves freedom, but is also fair and equitable.

Much political dialogue in the United States focuses on whether a particular practice is oppressive, or unfair, or inequitable. These are issues that Americans say they care about, and they would generally say that they oppose laws with these undesirable qualities. On a less celebratory note, one needs to remember that the Constitution as it existed before the Civil War Amendments—really, before the desegregation of society begun by *Brown v. Board of Education*[2]—did not count African Americans and other racial minorities as one of "us," and therefore justified legally depriving them of freedom, and fairness, and equity. That also reveals something about who Americans were, reinforcing racism and segregation in a way that still haunts the United States.

The laws of a society exert an important kind of influence on personal moral decisions. A part of each person's identity is derived from the laws of the society in which she lives. Such laws condition a person to be more accepting of the morality that is reflected in them, because that morality is the implicit backdrop of everyday life; it is generally taken for granted with little critical thought. Laws can help a people to fulfill their most noble aspirations, but laws also can blind them to the deepest meaning of those aspirations. For example, it has long been argued that the proslavery provisions of the original 1789 Constitution were necessary to secure ratification by the Southern colonies so as to create the United States as a genuine nation. It is undoubtedly true, however, that these provisions encouraged generations of Americans to ignore the plight of African Americans; certainly they did nothing to support the antislavery movement. Thus, they blinded Americans to a richer and fuller meaning of freedom and equality. Therefore, whether religious beliefs, along with moral beliefs in general, are properly present in the law-making process is a critically important question. Exclusion of religious beliefs skews the morality implied by our laws away from religious morality, and thereby exerts a subtle social pressure on religious people, implying to them that their beliefs are somehow wrong or, at least, out of step with the rest of society.

## MORALITY AND (DIS)RESPECT FOR LAW

The morality reflected in the laws governing the United States is an important source of personal and national identity. Perhaps more important, it is a potential limit on that identity. If religious and other moral considerations are out of place in politics, then the political process is only a referee mechanism for the accommodation of conflicting personal interests, rather than a process by which Americans arrive at consensus on how people should live together in the United States. Laws generated by the process are not thought to reflect any transcendent moral vision, or even any notions of right and wrong. Instead, laws represent only the relative political power of the interest groups that lobbied for their passage. If this is the case, then law-making is not a process by which the idea of America is created and re-created, but merely a value-neutral machine that measures raw political power by the equation, "might equals right."

Contrast, for example, the general American attitude toward tax evasion with that toward armed robbery. Prohibitions against the latter are certainly prudent rules for a civilized society. They might also be viewed as the natural result of the activities of politically powerful property owners who want the government to protect their possessions from forceful expropriation by less wealthy class enemies. Finally, laws against robbery reflect the widespread belief that depriving others of possessions by physical violence is simply wrong. Though violent crime is a serious problem in the United States, the vast majority of Americans are not criminally violent. This is so not merely because Americans know that such violence is illegal, or because they believe it is not in their best interests, but also (and, we believe, more importantly) because they believe it is wrong.

Income tax law, on the other hand, is a different matter altogether. Americans tend to view the Internal Revenue Code, particularly its details, as an artificial government construct which rests on no religious or other moral foundation. Those who are politically powerful succeed in shaping the Code to fit their personal financial needs; the rest of us pay as little as we can get away with. Most substantive commands of the Code—especially so-called tax "loopholes"—are morally arbitrary. They are the result of coalitions of political power rather than strongly held notions of right and wrong. The Code is not perceived to be linked to principles that will endure beyond the immediate present. Not surprisingly, noncompliance with the tax laws, even by otherwise law-abiding citizens, is widespread. Because the Code reflects no commitment to moral values that Americans share, it does not command their allegiance.

When law is viewed as the arbitrary outcome of the exercise of raw political power, rather than a search for those values that undergird the "good" society, it becomes vastly more difficult to persuade those subject to such law that it deserves their respect and obedience. This suggests that one can conceive of the decision whether to obey law in at least two ways. On one hand, the question of civil obedience might be seen as a matter of keeping faith with a moral vision which the citizen herself believes and shares. The critical issue in this context is whether the law reinforces a reality which the citizen considers worthy of respect and obedience—"Do I believe it is right and good to obey this law?" (Sometimes this question is generalized into whether it is right and good to obey laws in general, though one may not believe that the particular law in question is right and good.) On the other hand, the question might be a cynical calculation of personal prudence. In this context, the issue is whether obedience to the law will serve personal interests—"Will it help me to obey this law? Can I get away with disobeying it? What will the penalty be if I get caught?" The persuasive claims of morality disappear in favor of bald selfishness.

## LIBERALISM AND THE PRIVATIZATION OF RELIGION

In the United States, of course, all morality is not excluded from the political arena—only religious morality. It is not obvious why religious morality is considered unacceptably subjective and private, and secular morality is not. It may be a consequence of the basis of much modern secular moral theory. Such theory is often built on elaborations of the principle—made famous by the "invisible hand" of the 18th century political economist Adam Smith—that pursuing one's personal interests magically results in aggregate economic, social, and political decisions that are good for society as a whole. The implication is not only that one generally *will* choose one's self-interest in most situations, but also that one generally *should* do so, because it serves the common good as well as one's personal good.

Contemporary secular moral theory also often rests on relativism. Since ultimately there seems to be no way to demonstrate decisively what is good and right, government should avoid stands on value questions, leaving the resolution of those questions to the individual citizens themselves. This is a general characteristic of government in the liberal tradition stretching back to the 17th century philosopher Thomas Hobbes. Thus, secular morality, with its emphasis on personal preference and individual autonomy as sources of morality, may appear more consistent with liberal theories of government than does religious morality, with its common reliance on the judgment of the transcendent or divine.

At any rate, America does not suffer the full effects of a complete divorce between government and morality, because only religious modes of moral argument are prohibited. These effects seem to be further mitigated by the fact that much religious morality argues for the same kinds of substantive moral decisions and actions as secular morality, so that the exclusion of religious moral thinking in many cases seems unimportant. The political result desired by religious groups often is obtained, even though that result cannot be identified as resting on any religious foundation.

Nevertheless, the banishment of religion from politics, even if only implicit, exposes a central flaw of liberal political systems like that of the United States. At least since Descartes, who argued that there was a radical distinction between the essential natures of the mind and the body, Western intellectual thought has conceived of the world in dualisms or opposites. In contrast to Eastern thought, which more often emphasizes the unity and wholeness of the world, Western ways of learning focus on differences among the parts of the world, thereby fragmenting and compartmentalizing it.

As a Western political philosophy, liberalism likewise sees the world in conflicted, dualistic terms—rational versus irrational, objective versus subjective, public versus private, fact versus value, and, of course, secular versus religious. In liberal thought, the facets of an individual's personality are conceived of as being compartmentalized into various complementary categories that mirror the dualisms of Western knowledge. Each person, for example, has a public and a private identity. Public beliefs are those which are relevant to others; private beliefs have meaning only for the person and, perhaps, for the community that hold them. As we have discussed, religious belief is confined to the domain of the private.

Accordingly, religious belief can have no public meaning in liberal political theory; it is a mere taste or preference that lies beyond political analysis. Thus, one cannot talk about a "true" choice under liberal premises; one can only talk about "A's" choices and "B's" choices. To argue from religious premises in an arena of public life is, therefore, incoherent. It is like arguing that the color red is better-looking than the color blue, or that chocolate ice cream tastes better than vanilla. In a liberal society like the United States, religion belongs to the realm of the private and has no meaningful place in public life.

For the religious person, however, this division of herself into "public" and "private" is not easily accomplished; the commitment to religion is pervasive and all-encompassing. It is not a pose or affectation that can be dropped and picked up again at will. As theologian Paul Tillich wrote, "If religion is the state of being grasped by an ultimate concern, this state cannot be restricted to a special realm. The unconditional character of this concern implies that it refers to every moment of our life, to every space and every realm . . . . Essentially, the religious and the secular are not separated realms. Rather, they are within each other."[3] Similarly, Richard Neuhaus has observed that the liberal dualisms simply do not track how most people ordinarily relate to the world in which they live: "What people believe to be true and what people believe to be morally right are closely related. [T]he mutual dependence of fact and value is assumed."[4]

Most people simply do not divide the world up in the neat manner that liberal philosophy requires. Personal morality is unavoidably connected to American public life. To refer to our earlier examples, if a person believes that slaves or fetuses are fully human as a matter of fact, then for her slavery and abortion are morally evil. The fact that other people may think differently changes neither her moral premise—the "factual" conclusion about the definition of humanity—nor her moral outrage at the actions of others with conflicting definitions of humanity.

People do not think of themselves as religious one moment, and nonreligious the next; whether they consider themselves religious or nonreligious, they generally consider themselves to be so at all times and all places. Perhaps more important, Americans use their own personal

beliefs and morality to judge the actions of others when they find it
necessary and appropriate to do so.

Consider the political demise of Gary Hart, the leading contender for
the 1988 Democratic presidential nomination until his extramarital
escapades became widely known. The failure of his candidacy was
generally attributed to a previously unexposed vein of puritanism in the
contemporary American electorate. Try though he did, Hart simply could
not convince the voters that his private sexual exploits were not relevant
to his qualifications to hold high public office.

We believe that the reasons for Hart's political rejection had less to do
with puritanical morality than they did with the fact that most Democrats,
like most Americans, are not genuine liberals in the sense intended by
post-Enlightenment philosophy. They see a connection between a
politician's private life and his public aspirations, and demand some unity
between the two. Can a person truly be an exponent of gender equality,
as Hart purported to be, when he treats women as mere sex objects, as
Hart often did? Can one expect honesty and integrity in office from one
who so easily lied to cover a political liability, even if it was, as Hart
maintained, "none of our business"? The answers are obvious, and Hart
learned them the hard way. Most Americans have an intuition that the
public and the private are linked, not only in their own lives, but in the
lives of others as well. What a person might think and do publicly is
thought to depend at least in part on the kind of person she is privately.

When religious beliefs and religious morality are excluded from the
activities of public life, the religious individual who holds those beliefs
and subscribes to that morality is also excluded. She cannot use as a basis
for public action her religious individuality—those very thoughts, feelings, experiences, and beliefs that carry for her the greatest personal
meaning and thus that are most likely to move her to public action in the
first place. Yet the holistic, all-encompassing nature of religion makes it
difficult, if not impossible, for a religious person to set aside her religious
persona to participate in public life. Unless the religious individual
succeeds in disguising her religious motivations in the arguments of
secularism, most avenues of public life are closed to her.

## THE ALIENATION OF RELIGIOUS AMERICANS
## FROM PUBLIC LIFE

This exclusion of religious individuality from public life sets in motion
a powerful dynamic of alienation. If religious morality can influence law,
politics, and other aspects of American public life only when disguised

as secular morality, then the unmistakable message sent by the institutions and processes of public life is that religion is less legitimate than secularism, and less worthy of consideration by those who conduct the nation's business and interpret and preserve its public traditions. The knowledge that American public culture rejects the most authentic part of a religious individual's personality as wholly subjective and irrelevant to others makes her feel separated, illegitimate, and inferior. Such feelings erode the pride, loyalty, and support which a religious person might otherwise feel for American government and the culture and society it supports.

The stability of any liberal democracy depends on a perception of the people that their law treats everyone more or less equally and does not affirmatively dictate different results based upon the status of those that it governs. Liberal states that fail to cultivate this perception are either forced into authoritarianism or overthrown. The perception that one's government strives for justice, equality, and other principles widely shared by the people it governs is, after all, a powerful source of the conviction that government and its laws are worthy of one's protection and respect.

Political power cannot be effectively exercised without overwhelming coercion if it contradicts the deepest beliefs of those that it governs. A dramatic example was the declaration by Ferdinand Marcos of martial law in the Philippines in the 1960s. Although he was able to consolidate and extend his personal power for nearly a generation, he eventually had to flee the country when the price of controlling his adversaries rose to the level of wholesale slaughter. It is noteworthy that in the early 1980s, communist authorities in Poland were able to maintain their tenuous control of that country only through violent intimidation, including outright murder of anti-government activists. Yet even then, they could not maintain control. Equally worthy of note was the failure of the Shah of Iran to suppress or dilute the indigenous fundamentalism of Shiite Muslims while he tried to modernize Iran—a failure that led directly to his downfall.

People will not respect the values of a political system unless those values are validated by their own experience. Consider, as a particularly ironic example, the fundamentalist Christian right. Viciously criticized by Democrats and feared by more conventional Republicans, this latest version of political fundamentalism is in part the very creation of the mainstream political parties. When the members of fundamentalist denominations began to assert themselves politically in the 1970s, reacting to their perception of a pervasive public secularism which offended their deepest beliefs, their participation in the process was not welcomed. Accepting the fundamentalists as equal participants in the political arena and trying to speak to their concerns might have moderated their demands.

Instead, politicians at all points of the spectrum—although particularly those on the left—condemned this political activism. They saw the committed political activity by overtly and unapologetically religious people as a threat, since those who refuse to filter their beliefs through the screen of secularism cannot easily be accommodated in a public culture that is dominated by secular thinking. Faced with this reaction to their political activity, the fundamentalists understandably failed to see in conventional American politics any behavioral constraints which deserved their respect and obedience. On the contrary, the rejection of the fundamentalists by mainstream politicians radicalized the movement and encouraged its uncritical use of raw political power to achieve fundamentalist objectives.

Although recently the religious right has moderated its style some-what, if not its agenda, it has done so on its own; political success encouraged *it* to reach out to other groups, rather than vice versa, in an attempt to build a more comprehensive political coalition. Thus, the Democrats and the Republicans helped to create the very religious monster they warned against. ("Invoking the nightmares we fear," as Neuhaus puts it.[5]) They can hardly complain now that the fundamentalists are illegitimate political actors because they do not play by the conventional (secular) political rules.

The radicalization of the Christian right is just one example of the disaffection of religious people that will occur unless the custodians of American public life accept religion as a legitimate public actor. If the religious people who constitute so much of the American populace come to believe, as many already do, that the political process does not respect their religious beliefs to the same extent that it respects secular beliefs, then they themselves will respect neither that process nor the laws and culture that it perpetuates. Their alienation from public culture will inevitably lead to their radicalization and, potentially, to their revolt.

Incredible as revolution may sound, it is not wholly beyond the realm of possibility. Noting that most conflicts since World War II have had a significant religious element, religious historian Martin Marty has observed that "it is as likely that World War III will erupt over religious issues as any other."[6] Marty goes on: "The age of tolerance and enlightenment, which was late, brief, and fragile, yet taken for granted in much of Europe and Anglo-America, may very well be passing. I cannot think of any place in the world where empathy, responsiveness, or 'counter-intolerance' in religion is growing. In a crowded, weapons-filled world, I consider that dangerous."[7]

Should religious violence erupt in the United States, government would have to respond with force necessary to put down the rebellion, if it wished to survive. Such a conflict would be ghastly. One need only look to the history of the European Reformation to appreciate the destruction and violence—cultural as well as physical—that accompanies religious war. Moreover, the possibility would remain that peace could not be restored, or that a radical religious movement could succeed in overthrowing our existing constitutional system and replace it with some fundamentalist religious sovereign.[8] Again, history teaches that the unification of government power with sectarian belief is deeply oppressive.

We think that religious revolution in the United States is unlikely, if barely possible. But the way stations between violent revolution and peaceful political dissent are numerous; a society can be undermined by less than violence. One can ignore convention and depart from tradition, as the religious right has done in the political arena. If the convention is civility, and the tradition political tolerance, then the results of such ignorance and dissent can be politically and socially alarming even thought they fall well short of revolutionary violence.

Excluding a large social group like religious people from the main-stream processes of politics and public life will inevitably lead to conflict and polarization between religion and secularism. The fault line between private religion and public secularism which has been exploited by the religious right indicates a point of collision between two powerful and important social forces in the United States. Although it appears improbable that the collision will generate an earthquake, it nevertheless deserves serious attention.

America must deal with religion one way or the other. It may accept religion as an equal and legitimate participant in law, politics, and other aspects of public life—which is the course we will argue for in the following chapters. If it does not, however, it must prepare to put down attempts by disaffected religious people and organizations to dominate or to circumvent the public institutions and processes that exclude them. In either event, one thing is certain: Religion as a force in American public life will be here to be dealt with for some time to come.

## NOTES

1. Walz v. Tax Commission, 397 U.S. 664, 694, 695 (1970) (concurring opinion).
2. 349 U.S. 294 (1955); 347 U.S. 483 (1954).
3. Paul Tillich, *Theology of Culture*, ed. Robert C. Kimball (New York: Oxford University Press, 1978), 41.
4. Richard John Neuhaus, *The Naked Public Square: Religion and Democracy in America*, 2d ed. (Grand Rapids, Mich.: Eerdmans, 1986), 180.
5. Ibid., 177 (chapter title).
6. Martin Marty, "The Reporting of Religious Events by the Media: A Framework for Inquiry" in *The Religion Beat: The Reporting of Religion in the Media*. Conference Report (New York: The Rockefeller Foundation, 1981), 8, 15.
7. Ibid.
8. Cf. Margaret Atwood, *The Handmaid's Tale* (New York: Ballantine, 1985).

Part II

# The Alienation of Religion
# from American Public Life

# Chapter 3

# Religion and the Secular

How did public life come to be so secular while private life remained so religious? The origins of the secular society reach back centuries into European history. During the Middle Ages, the union of church and state was taken for granted. Accordingly, until the Reformation in the 16th century, religion and government were unified, each representing a different aspect of the same divine authority. After the Reformation, however, Europe began an institutional disengagement of religion and government that was propelled by both theological and political forces. Moreover, beginning with the Enlightenment or "Age of Reason" in the 17th century, Europe also began to replace religious belief with scientific knowledge as the better way to understand the world. As a consequence of both the Reformation and Enlightenment, many European thinkers rejected the medieval union of church and state, concluding that the church should not control the government, the government should not corrupt the church, and neither should have the power to coerce religious belief.

In the United States, the influence of these events in Europe is evidenced by the religion clauses of the First Amendment to the American Constitution: "Congress shall make no law respecting an establishment of religion, or prohibiting the free exercise thereof. . . ." The first phrase has become known as the "establishment clause," and the second as the "free exercise clause." The religion clauses embody the twin notions that religious belief and practice are matters of individual conscience beyond the reach of government, and that the church and the state should refrain from intruding upon one another's affairs.

Following the American revolution into the 19th and early 20th centuries, the United States moved away from sectarian public discourse towards a more secular language that mediated the cultural and religious diversity created by increased education, industrialization, and immigration. By the 1930s, the United States had inherited the full legacy of the Enlightenment. The pragmatic move away from sectarian language in service to cultural and political unity was transformed into a normative preference of secularism among intellectual elites as the language of progress and learning. The secular society had arrived.

## INSTITUTIONAL SEPARATION IN REFORMATION EUROPE

Secularism began with the distillation of two separate spheres of institutional influence within European society as a result of the Reformation. One sphere became the domain of the spiritual, ruled by the church; the other the domain of the secular, ruled by the state. At this time, the word "secular" merely described property previously owned by the church which had been legally transferred to individuals or government for nonecclesiastical uses.[1] The meaning of the word eventually broadened into a general description of all institutions that were not related to the church. Prior to the Reformation, however, the concepts "religious" and "secular" did not exist as descriptions of fundamentally different aspects of society. Although there clearly were tension and conflict in the relations between church and state during this time, the state was not considered to be nonreligious. Both church and state were part of the Christian foundation upon which medieval society was built. There were two forces that encouraged the institutional separation of church and state into fundamentally different spheres of the religious and the secular; one force was theological, the other political.

### Theological Separationism

The church of the Middle Ages had fallen heir to the classical idea that "the purpose of the state was to establish and conserve a complete and finished program of life."[2] It was committed to a theology in which all of society was united through the spiritual leadership of the church and the divinely sanctioned rule of kings and princes. Thus, although early Christian theologians like Augustine had written of separate spiritual and temporal spheres of social life, they did not understand these spheres to be *fundamentally* different—that is, the state was not understood to be nonreligious, but was simply a different aspect of the sovereign authority of God. For Augustine, "there was not one body of men who formed the state and one which formed the church, for all men were included in both. There was only a single Christian society . . . and it included . . . the whole world."[3] In other words, religious and political authority, although distinct in some respects, were each derived from the same divine source. Thus, they were merely complementary aspects of the same authority that ordered all of society, in much the same way that the executive power of the American Presidency and the legislative power of Congress are distinct aspects of the same sovereign authority of the United States of America.

Augustine's theology was eventually eclipsed by that of Thomas Aquinas. Drawing on Aristotle's conception of the world as a unified whole, Aquinas taught that the spiritual and the temporal were bound together in "a universal synthesis, an all-embracing system, the keynote of which was harmony and conciliance."[4] Aquinas's position led him to conclude that even those social institutions of the Middle Ages administered primarily by nonecclesiastical rulers, such as the complex feudal system of rights and obligations extending from the king down to the lowest serf, were divinely sanctioned even though they were not part of the ecclesiastical hierarchy.

The violence and oppression that were facts of medieval life made harmony and reconciliation unlikely frameworks for analyzing social life. Accordingly, theologians of the late Middle Ages and the early Reformation returned to the Augustinian separation of the spiritual and the temporal. This time, however, the separation was made more fundamental. Philosopher Alasdair MacIntyre states that in the late Middle Ages, the synthesis of the spiritual and the temporal advocated by Aquinas was "replaced by an appeal to divine revelation and to mystical experience," which together emphasized the "distance between God and man."[5] The idea that religion and government inhabited fundamentally different realms was further elaborated during the Reformation. The two most important Reformation theologians, Martin Luther and John Calvin, both argued that God had instituted two kingdoms on earth: one spiritual, to be administered by the church; and the other temporal, to be ruled by a civil sovereign.

As the Reformation wore on, civil rulers lost their aura of divine legitimacy, becoming instead mere facts of political life with no necessary connection to God. The division of society into qualitatively different religious and nonreligious realms received its strongest theological support from certain Protestant sects of the late Reformation, such as the

Anabaptists in Europe—ancestors of the Amish and Mennonite sects—
and the separatist Puritans in England. The Anabaptists believed in literal
withdrawal from worldly society in order to live according to the purity
and perfection of God's revealed word in the Bible. The separatist
Puritans wished to purge the church of corrupt and coercive worldly
practices which they believed were the result of government maintenance
of the established Church of England.

In the view of both Anabaptists and Puritans, unity or alignment of
the church with civil government unavoidably corrupted the church and
stained the religious conscience of its believers. The only solution that
seemed to them to preserve the religious integrity of the church and its
believers was separation of their religious activities of devotion and
worship from the political activities of government. Thus, both Anabaptists and Puritans incorporated a theological principle of church–
state separation.

### Religious Pluralism

The "Reformation" is an ironic name for the revolution sparked by
Luther, since far more was destroyed by the Reformation than was
reformed by it.[6] Despite the threat of torture by the Inquisition, the heresy
of Protestantism spread throughout Europe. Moreover, it quickly became
clear that the heretics themselves often disagreed as violently with each
other as they did with Rome. A prince who established, say, Lutheranism
as the state religion within his realm had to contend with unrest not only
from the Catholics among his subjects, but also from non-Lutheran
Protestant dissenters. No longer could civil government assume that
society rested on any sort of religious consensus; the Reformation
"fragment[ed] moral authority in the modern world."[7]

This moral fragmentation marked the birth of something the Western
world now takes for granted—religious pluralism. In the 16th century,
however, pluralism was a new phenomenon that posed a serious challenge
to the ability of the emerging nation-states of Europe to govern their
subjects. As the Protestant Reformation and the Catholic Counter-Ref-
ormation contended throughout Europe, kings and princes chose sides
by establishing either Catholicism or one of the new Protestant sects as
the official state religion of their respective realms. Although dissenters
from the state religion were sometimes tolerated, this was the exception
rather than the rule, especially in the early days of the Reformation. This
meant that obedience to the crown usually had a theological as well as a
political dimension: One who obeyed the king was perceived as recog-

nizing not only the civil authority of the king to govern the realm, but also the religious authority of the church or sect with which the king had aligned his domain.

So long as obedience to civil authority retained a religious dimension, one could count on massive civil disobedience on the part of dissenters from the state religion. The ability of civil government to enforce the law and command the respect of its subjects would be in doubt. Protestant Huguenots in 16th and 17th century France, for example, resisted royal authority because the French king was closely allied with the pope. Most Huguenots would not have objected to obeying the king's command had he been perceived as a purely civil sovereign. However, because he was also seen as the agent of Rome, obeying the king constituted obedience to the pope as well, to which no Huguenot would willingly consent.

A similar problem existed in Elizabethan England, where Anglican bishops sat in the House of Lords as a matter of right, and the established Anglican church had great influence on the nature and content of civil laws. This enraged the Puritan dissenters, and contributed to their widespread disobedience of laws which they perceived to have been enacted as the result of Anglican pressure and influence. The new religious pluralism that now existed in most of Europe demanded that civil and ecclesiastical authority be separated if the state was not to spend extraordinary resources merely to maintain civil law and order.

For both theological and political reasons, then, the catholic unity of church and state on which European society had rested for nearly a thousand years eventually disappeared. Although by the end of the 18th century the established state church was still the rule for the nations of Europe, most of them, by law or custom, had reached accommodations with religious dissenters which recognized their existence and occasionally even granted them limited political and civil rights. With this tacit recognition that secular government had no jurisdiction over religious conscience, widespread civil disobedience eventually ceased. The Reformation thus yielded the first condition for creation of the secular society, namely, the conceptualization of church and state as inhabiting fundamentally separate spheres of social and political life.

## INSTITUTIONAL SEPARATION IN AMERICA

Pluralism presented an even greater problem for the United States than it did for Europe. The various colonies had been settled by culturally and ethnically diverse groups of people. Difficulties of travel and communication in the 17th and 18th centuries ensured that the colonies would develop generally different ways of living and thinking rather than melding their differences into a common culture. This cultural diversity was a fact of colonial religious life as well. The Congregationalists of New England reflected the strict Calvinism of their Puritan forebears, while the Anglican establishment of England was strongest in Virginia and the other Southern colonies. Maryland was settled by Roman Catholics. Baptists, Presbyterians, and Methodists, and to a lesser extent Catholics and Jews, were sprinkled throughout all of the colonies, with perhaps the most diverse religious populations residing in Rhode Island and in the mid-Atlantic colonies of New York and New Jersey.

Toward the end of the 18th century, the influence of the Enlightenment was felt in the proliferation of deism among intellectuals like Benjamin Franklin, Thomas Jefferson, and Thomas Paine, who were suspicious of traditional religion, and who believed in a rather vague deity which intervened in human affairs, if at all, only according to rationally explainable "natural" laws. It was due in no small part to the religious diversity of the colonies that the Bill of Rights contained unprecedented provisions guaranteeing freedom of religious conscience and prohibiting the establishment of a national church.

As if the religious diversity of the 18th century were not enough, the Second Great Awakening exploded upon the American scene in the early 19th century. This period saw the resurgence of Protestant fundamental-ism, with the multiplication of Protestant sects almost beyond number, and the formation of numerous experimental religious communities. This period also saw the birth of distinctly American religions like Christian Science and Mormonism.

By the midpoint of the 19th century, it had become clear that no single religious sect would ever dominate the American cultural scene; there were simply too many denominations for any one to rise above the rest. As a consequence, there was no single denominational language that was adequate to the task of communication among such a theologically diverse population. Of necessity, Americans began to move toward a less sectarian language in public life, one that was not associated with any particular Protestant denomination. It was only by using a more secular language that one could carry on public business and dialogue without importing into the discussion the divisive theological differences that were reflected in the distinct voices of the innumerable American sects. "Secular" gradually came to be associated with "religiously neutral."

The move away from sectarian language as the preferred American language of public discourse in the 19th century did not immediately signal the end of public religious influence or discourse. In the first place, there was no explicit 19th century ethic that required the divorce of religion from politics and government; on the contrary, both churches and individuals actively intervened on behalf of self-consciously religious agenda well into the 20th century.

There was no clear division of society into spheres of the religious and the secular in the 19th century; rather, religion and government emerged as competing centers of institutional authority, each of which recognized the preeminence of the other only in certain matters. In 19th century America, this meant that as a matter of both custom and law, the government could not interfere in the internal affairs of the church, and the church likewise was prohibited from writing its theology into law to be enforced by the government.[8] For the individual citizen, however, no such limits existed. While government could not coerce religious *belief*, it was perfectly free to regulate and even to prohibit religiously motivated *action* whenever it was thought desirable for public safety or welfare.[9] By the same token, it was both legally and culturally acceptable for individuals to argue public policy in explicitly religious, even sectarian, terms, and many did so. Indeed, the abolitionist movement of the early part of the 19th century and the Progressive movement of the latter part of the century were both decisively influenced by groundswells of religious fundamentalism.

By the 1930s, however, politicians had discovered that maximizing their political appeal to a diverse religious population in an industrial society required that they mute the sectarian element of their message. A politician who needed votes from a religiously diverse electorate could best succeed if he used a language that appealed to all without offending any. This move away from sectarian language was encouraged by the dramatic increase in immigration from Europe during the second half of the 19th century, which added significant numbers of Catholics and Jews to the diversity of Protestant sects that already existed among Americans. Thus, the move away from sectarianism toward secularism in public discourse was inspired, not by any Enlightenment belief that the separation of church and state required more than the institutional separation of the Reformation, but rather by the pragmatic instinct that a more secular public discourse was essential to political success.

The move away from sectarianism toward secularism likewise did not obscure the fact that Americans remained generally Protestant despite the recent influx of non-Protestant immigrants. However, seemingly limitless sectarian differences among American Protestants restricted even this influence to general manifestations that would not provoke theological argument among the Protestant majority, such as extolling the virtues of hard work and individualism, or appropriating biblical images like William Jennings Bryan's famous "cross of gold."

While religious imagery remained acceptable and influential in American public life, the need to keep such imagery at a high level of generality diluted much of its rhetorical power. Perhaps more important, it necessarily restricted theologically meaningful religious discourse to private life, outside of the public realm of law, politics, and government. Vague references to deity, expiation, forgiveness, and charity, typified by Lincoln's Second Inaugural Address, began to delineate the boundary of effective religious discourse in public. Sectarian discourse became increasingly confined to private life, and ultimately survived in public life only as "civil religion"—faintly Protestant platitudes which reaffirmed the religious base of American culture despite being largely devoid of theological significance.[10]

Thus, Protestantism still affected public business, but implicitly; more as the source and background of political movements than as the movements themselves. This religious influence has become known as the "de facto Protestant establishment."[11] Public schools read from the King James Bible and emphasized individuality rather than community in judgment and action, practices which eventually caused Catholics to withdraw from the public school system. A similar Protestant piety was reflected in the solidification of customs such as legislative prayer and recognition of Thanksgiving, Christmas, and Easter holidays. States outlawed blasphemy, punished atheism, and enforced the Christian Sabbath.

The resurgence of political activity by religious fundamentalists in the latter part of the 19th century and the early part of the 20th put government authority behind temperance, anti-evolution, and anti-polygamy laws. These laws and actions often were not defended in theological terms—as necessary, for example, to building the kingdom of God on earth—but rather in more secular terms, as necessary to building and maintaining a well-ordered, "civilized" society.[12]

The 19th and early 20th centuries in the United States, then, were characterized by a curious melding of religion and government in American public life which seems contradictory to contemporary notions of church–state separation, but which made perfect sense to the Protestant culture of the time. To the 19th century American Protestant, the separation of church and state demanded by the Reformation and the Enlightenment was merely institutional. That separation was honored throughout the country not only by the prohibition of the First Amendment establishment clause on government support of any particular sect as the national church, but also by political decisions in all of the states not to establish particular sects as state religions. Religious and secular authority were allied in a variety of ways, but in a subtle and diffuse sense.

As the United States moved from the 19th century into the 20th, the justifications for such alliances were increasingly presented in secular rather than theological terms. The pragmatic move from sectarianism toward secularism in search of a religiously neutral public discourse left public discourse caught between sectarian and secular language. It would not remain long in this awkward and unstable state, however. The move towards a more secular public discourse with broader, nonsectarian appeal sowed the seeds of a more fundamental limitation on public discourse which bore fruit in the 20th century.

## THE TRIUMPH OF THE ENLIGHTENMENT

Reformation Protestants, whether as dissenters or as the established church, were every bit as uncompromising and fanatical as their Catholic predecessors. Protestants and Catholics alike persecuted, tortured, and killed people for their failure to confess orthodox beliefs. So blindly and completely did the adherents to different religious sects hate that each persisted in decades-long attempts to exterminate the others, culminating in the mindless carnage of the Thirty Years War in continental Europe and a century of violence in England caused by Henry VIII, his daughter Mary, and the Puritan Revolution. This bloodshed, of course, was in addition to the ever-present oppression of Jews and other non-Christians.

To the 17th century intellectual, then, religion was a scourge, whether it was Protestant or Catholic. It had become a violent and destabilizing enterprise that put the world on a backwards course. Richard Neuhaus writes that "the wars of religion of the 16th and 17th centuries have left an indelible mark upon Western political thought and practice. From that experience we presumably learned that particularist religion is an impossibly divisive dynamic, destroying the foundations of the *polis* it would control. Still in the 19th century profound thinkers were operating from the memory of religion's ambition and ability to dominate."[13]

Accordingly, the ethic that grew out of the secular Enlightenment was that reason, education, and science held the key to civilization and progress. When considered against the order of the newly discovered Newtonian universe, the dogmatism, violence, and fanaticism that seemed to have accompanied 16th and 17th century religion stamped it as a dangerous superstition. The Enlightenment project was to apply the tools of reason and science to the truth claims of religion, proving them false and thereby liberating society from the intellectual oppression and political instability that religion perpetuated. Freed from the restraining influence of unreasonable and undemonstrable beliefs, society could progress to a more tolerant and enlightened state. Eighteenth century French philosopher Claude-Adrien Helvetius, for example, believed in "almost limitless possibilities of transforming human nature, if only political despotism and ecclesiastical obscurantism did not prevent radical reform of the educational system."[14] This meant that the author-itarianism of both Catholic and early Protestant theology was subjected to severe criticism. Whereas those theologies insisted that the command-ments be respected because they issued from God, and that clerics and rulers be obeyed because they represented God on earth, Enlightenment thinkers required reasonable and increasingly empirical explanations for such obedience and respect. When the churches could not supply such naturalistic explanations for their beliefs, they became intellectually discredited.

The Enlightenment reached full flower in the United States during the 20th century. Its effect is most dramatically illustrated by the response of American religion to the intellectual challenge of Darwin's theory of natural selection. Protestant theology at the turn of the century pre-supposed the divine creation *ex nihilo*—literally, "from nothing"—of the earth and all of its plants, animals, and human inhabitants. Life was, therefore, not an accident, but a conscious gift of God. Although Darwinian evolution had nothing explicit to say about God, its proposi-tion that life adapted and survived through random mutations seemed clearly to contradict the idea of divine order embedded in the traditional creation narrative. The further suggestion that humans had descended from lower forms of life added further insult to religious believers, who thought of themselves as children of God, not chimpanzees.

Most religious leaders and their followers, especially conservatives, flatly rejected evolution as an explanation of the origin of biological life. But natural selection was a powerful idea; it quickly spread from biology to other intellectual disciplines. In literature, for example, critics quickly developed a Darwinist theory of genre development by analogizing literary works to a biological species. Thus, the literary works best suited to their social and political environments were those that prospered and survived. In the social sciences, Darwinism suggested that inequalities inherent in existing social arrangements were the inevitable result of randomly distributed talents and abilities. Thus, protective legislation designed to mitigate the effects of these inequalities was not only unnecessary, it was undesirable. In this view, protecting weaker and less talented people, rather than permitting them to die off, would dilute the gene pool; without legal protection, only the tougher and more talented would survive and reproduce, thereby strengthening and perpetuating those human traits most helpful to social and economic success. Indeed, Darwin's theory has a strong Calvinist flavor, which made its rejection by religious conservatives more than a little ironic.

In any event, such an influential and powerful idea would not be defeated merely by an appeal to tradition; an equally powerful intellectual alternative was needed to compete with natural selection if religion was successfully to withstand the Darwinist assault upon traditional beliefs. An intellectually competitive alternative, however, was not forthcoming. In a famous legal action under Tennessee's anti-evolution law, *Scopes v. State*,15 the champion of conservative Protestants, William Jennings Bryan, was humiliated on the witness stand by Scopes's lawyer, Clarence Darrow, when Bryan attempted to defend the plausibility of divine creation as recorded in Genesis. Religion won the battle in that case— Scopes was convicted of teaching evolution in violation of the law—but it lost the war when Bryan's inability to answer the intellectual challenge of evolution was widely reported. To the extent that they were inconsistent with Darwinian evolution, religious beliefs about divine creation were publicly discredited.

The conflict between evolution and fundamentalist religion was typical of how science displaced religion in American public life during the 20th century. Historian Edward Purcell writes that during this era,

> the idea of the middle ages, dominated by scholastic philosophy, an authoritarian church, and a hierarchical social order, emerged as the preeminent symbol of everything that was bad in human society. . . . Science, gaining strength since the seventeenth century, and finally able to discredit those "Dark Ages," was inextricably tied up in the minds of most intellectuals with everything that was best in human society.16

Subsequent events further undermined religion. In the decade before World War II, Americans became disenchanted with religious fundamentalism, a political attitude symbolized by the repeal of Prohibition in 1933 a few years after the *Scopes* trial. The war itself included bloody conflicts with Nazi Germany and Fascist Italy, two dictatorships characterized by the union of potent political ideologies with the machinery of government. Immediately following the war came the global ideological conflict between the United States and Soviet communism, an adversary seemingly in the same mold as Hitler and Mussolini. In this climate, the lesson that ideological passion, including religious belief, ought to be discarded in favor of reason and science was an easy one to learn. The superstitions of religion had finally been overcome.

Today, there is a serious cultural division between religion (especially conservative religion) and intellectual life. Indeed, the term "fundamentalist" is generally taken to be a synonym for "anti-intellectual," and even so-called "liberal" denominations are not taken seriously by intellectuals to the extent that they cling to beliefs in genuine divinity.[17] Faithfulness to the ideal of the secular society predominates among American intellectuals, and an aggressive secularism pervades American intellectual life. Law professor James Boyd White has noted

> a peculiar division between academic and religious thought in our culture. In the academic world, we tend to speak as though all participants in our conversation were purely rational actors engaged in rational debate; perhaps some people out there in the world are sufficiently benighted that they turn to religious beliefs or other superstitions, but that is not true of us or, if it is true, we hide it, and it ought not to be true of them. Ours is a secular academy and, we think, a secular state.[18]

Similarly, law professor Kent Greenawalt has written that "a good many professors and other intellectuals display a hostility or skeptical indifference to religion that amounts to a thinly disguised contempt for belief in any reality beyond that discoverable by scientific inquiry and ordinary human experience."[19] This attitude is particularly widespread among those who teach at American law schools.[20]

Just as the national media have contributed to the perception that religion is not relevant to politics in the United States, as we discussed in chapter 1, so also American literary critics, sociologists, political scientists, legal academics, and other intellectuals have helped to create the erroneous impression that the United States and its people are discarding religion as a significant force in their lives. It is no doubt reinforced by the anti- or areligious bias of the intellectual fathers of modern sociology—Herbert Spencer, Karl Marx, Emile Durkheim, Max Weber, and Georg Simmel[21]—as well as by a relative lack of interest in the study of religion by American political scientists as compared to other, secular influences on the political system.[22] Political scientist James Reichley marvels at the persistence of religious belief in the United States despite "recent incursions by civil humanism among cultural elites. . . ."[23]

In the 20th century, then, religious discourse lost its ability to compete intellectually with secular discourse in public contexts. It went from being merely less effective in the 19th century to being ineffective and disrespected in the 20th. Public life went on without religion, although Americans remained religiously faithful in private. As we have described, religion in the United States remains vital, involved, and animated. The reality is that secularization accurately describes only contemporary *public* life in the United States.

## NOTES

1. Hans Kung, *On Being a Christian*, trans. Edward Quinn (New York: Doubleday, 1976), 26–27.

2. A. D. Lindsay, *Religion, Science, and Society in the Modern World* (New Haven: Yale University Press, 1943), 7.

3. George Sabine, *A History of Political Theory*, rev. ed. (New York: Holt, Rinehart & Winston, 1950), 225.

4. Ibid., 248.

5. Alasdair MacIntyre, *A Short History of Ethics* (New York: Macmillan, 1966), 119.

6. See *The Columbia History of the World*, ed. John A. Garraty and Peter Gay (New York: Harper & Row, 1972), 518–19.

7. Richard John Neuhaus, *The Naked Public Square: Religion and Democracy in America*, 2d ed. (Grand Rapids, Mich.: Eerdmans, 1986), 174.

8. E.g., Watson v Jones, 80 U.S. (13 Wall.) 679 (1871).

9. E.g., Reynolds v. United States, 98 U.S. 108 (1878). Law professor Michael McConnell has recently cast doubt on the proposition that the belief-action distinction was settled law when *Reynolds* was decided. See Michael McConnell, "The Origins and Historical Understanding of the Free Exercise of Religion," *Harvard Law Review* 103 (1990): 1409.

10. Cf. Robert N. Bellah, *The Broken Covenant: American Civil Religion in Time of Trial* (New York: Seabury Press, 1975).

11. Mark De Wolfe Howe, *The Garden and the Wilderness* (Chicago: University of Chicago Press, 1965), 11.

12. E.g., Reynolds v. United States, 98 U.S. 145, 166–67 (1878).

13. Neuhaus, *Naked Public Square*, 156.

14. MacIntyre, *History of Ethics*, 181.

15. 154 Tenn 105, 289 S.W. 363 (1927).

16. Edward A. Purcell, Jr., *The Crisis of Democratic Theory: Scientific Naturalism and the Problem of Value* (Lexington: University Press of Kentucky, 1973), 61.

17. Neuhaus, *Naked Public Square*, ch. 13.

18. James Boyd White, "Response to Roger Cramton's Article," *Journal of Legal Education* 37 (1987): 533.

50 The Alienation of Religion

19. Kent Greenawalt, *Religious Convictions and Political Choice* (New York: Oxford University Press, 1988), 6.

20. See ibid., 5; Michael J. Perry, *Morality, Politics, and Law: A Bicentennial Essay* (New York: Oxford University Press, 1988), 10, 211 n.10; Roger Cramton, "Beyond the Ordinary Religion," *Journal of Legal Education* 37 (1987): 509; Rex Lee, "The Role of the Religious Law School," *Villanova Law Review* 30 (1985): 1175; Peter Shane, "Prophets and Provocateurs," *Journal of Legal Education* 37 (1987): 529.

21. Theodore Caplow, Howard Bahr, and Bruce Chadwick, *All Faithful People: Change and Continuity in Middletown's Religion* (Minneapolis: University of Minnesota Press, 1983), 31–32.

22. Peter Benson and Dorothy Williams, *Religion on Capitol Hill: Myths and Realities* (New York: Oxford University Press, 1986), 5.

23. A. James Reichley, *Religion in American Public Life* (Washington, D.C.: Brookings Institute, 1985), 360.

# Chapter 4

# Religion and the Unconscious

The 20th century has seen extraordinary advances in knowledge about the human mind. In particular, much has been learned about the "unconscious" mind—that portion of the human brain that functions without our being aware of what it is doing. According to Carl Jung, manifestations of the unconscious mind include "all urges, impulses, and intentions; all perceptions and intuitions; all rational or irrational thoughts, conclusions, inductions deductions, and premises; and all varieties of feeling."[1] Despite this advance in knowledge, contemporary society still has difficulty dealing with ideas and concepts that are tied to experiences beyond human consciousness. Dreams, visions, voices, insights, and other human experiences with roots in the unconscious mind are still often treated as evidence of mental illness or other disorders.

The unconscious mind need not be treated as a manifestation of disease. It is a vast reservoir of ideas and images that are a rich resource of human meaning in their own right. These ideas and images are one means by which humans conceptualize the world. Accordingly, they form a foundation of human existence. Manifestations of the unconscious are critically important to understanding motivations for human behavior at both the individual and the social level. In particular, they carry important implications for the exclusion of religion from American public life. The religious experience, with its spiritual, extrarational character, is closely related to manifestations of the unconscious, which by definition are difficult to explain by reference to conscious understanding. This failure to treat the unconscious mind as a legitimate source of meaning that is available to everyone obscures the tremendous force that the unconscious mind exerts on all members of society, and further alienates religious people from public life.

## THE UNCONSCIOUS MIND AS A SOURCE OF KNOWLEDGE

Modern humanity has long been aware of the processes of conscious experience—study, recall, synthesis, reflection, and so on. However, in this century psychologists have determined that the mind takes in and stores many more things than the conscious mind can recall or comprehend. Freud, Jung, and others postulated and described a part of the mind that captures and records experiences that are not explainable—that are not even known—by the conscious mind. These extrarational and unknown experiences are registered and stored in the "unconscious" portion of the mind. The thoughts, images, and impressions of these experiences, though obscured from consciousness, nevertheless exert considerable influence on it.

The unconscious mind is not bound by conventions of rationality or common experience, as is the conscious mind. The unconscious mind pays no attention to time and space; it does not differentiate past, present, and future, as the conscious mind does; and it is similarly unconcerned about geographic place. Thus, manifestations of the unconscious commonly mix characters and images that come from different chronologies or cultures. Dreams, for example, often have no sense of normal time or place. The dreamer finds herself first in one place, then instantaneously in another. Things that happen in dreams often have no correlate in everyday life. According to Jung,

> a dream is quite unlike a story told by the conscious mind. In everyday life one thinks out what one wants to say, selects the most telling way of saying it, and tries to make one's remarks logically coherent. . . . But dreams have a different texture. Images that seem contradictory and ridiculous crowd in on the dreamer, the normal sense of time is lost, and commonplace things can assume a fascinating or threatening aspect.[2]

The unconscious mind confronts one as baffling precisely because its manifestations do not "make sense." It is this nonsensical, extrarational attribute of the unconscious mind that makes it such a valuable part of human knowledge and understanding. Unconscious images may not make sense, but they are impressed upon the conscious mind in ways that are nonetheless real. Everyone has had a "crazy" dream that was so frighteningly vivid as to seem real. Manifestations of the unconscious mind frequently push themselves upon a person in the form of dreams, visions, hunches, insights, feelings, and even voices. In the context of everyday conscious life, these illogical and irrational experiences are habitually ignored and discarded, because they are inconsistent with the way modern humanity (in the West, at least) is conditioned to understand the world. It is a quintessentially modern attribute to ignore or to discount phenomena that fall beyond the bounds of reason or ordinary human experience.

If these manifestations of unconscious thought are taken seriously, however, they force one to think about what they could mean, even if the experiences seem not to make sense in terms of conscious experiences. By manifesting startling and unlikely images and events in such a way that they seem nonetheless real, the unconscious mind illuminates subtle aspects of human life by bringing to one's conscious attention things she otherwise would ignore, reject, or misunderstand.

Ironically, manifestations of the unconscious mind have played an important role in uncovering knowledge in that most rational of human endeavors, physical science. Jung argued that "even physics, the strictest of all applied sciences, depends to an astonishing degree upon intuition . . . . "[3] The 19th century German chemist August Kekulé ascribed his important discovery of the closed molecular structure of the benzene ring to a bizarre dream in which atoms and molecules appeared in the form of snakes. He describes how in his dream,

> the atoms danced before my eyes; now my mind's eye distinguished larger formations of manifold shapes; long rows, often more tightly joined. Everything was in motion, writhing and coiling in serpentine fashion, and lo and behold . . . what was this? One serpent grasped its own tail, and mockingly that thing whirled before my eyes . . . the benzol ring! I spent the rest of the night elaborating the consequences of the theory.[4]

The unconscious mind, then, can be as much a source of knowledge and understanding as the conscious mind. In fact, it is a far richer source than the conscious mind of the symbols that influence human life. Symbols are shorthand representations of important facets of the individual and collective lives of a people. A symbol always suggests more than its obvious, immediate meaning, capturing in a single expression, design, or object some truth about human life. Much of this meaning is accessible only through the unconscious. Symbols are not constructed through a process familiar to the conscious mind; cultural symbols and their meaning emanate from the unconscious, so that people respond to and understand a valid symbol of their culture without, at first thought, knowing why. Jung compared cultural symbols to prejudices. Both evoke a deep emotional response that often seems beyond the ability of the individual to control.

For example, the cross powerfully represents to Christians the central doctrines and events of Christianity—Jesus's life, his crucifixion, his atonement for sins, his resurrection, his prophecied return. Although the power of this symbol is evident, the exact source of its hold on people is difficult to pinpoint. The central beliefs of Christianity are neither rational nor empirical. The story of Jesus's life is fantastic, even fanciful, by the measure of science. (Bertrand Russell poked fun at the Christian doctrine of the universal resurrection by wondering how God might reconstruct the corporeal elements of cannibals and their victims.[5]) Yet strong belief in the divinity of Jesus persists. The source and strength of this belief are drawn from the unconscious mind to the surface of human consciousness by the symbol of the cross.

## CONSCIOUSNESS AND UNCONSCIOUSNESS

Psychiatrists and psychologists have developed innumerable theories attempting to explain the relation between the conscious mind and its unconscious counterpart, ranging from the mundane to the epic. One early theory suggested that the symbols emanating from the unconscious mind are correlated with the foods one eats, recalling Ebenezer Scrooge, who thought he was suffering from indigestion upon being confronted with Jacob Marley's ghost. "You may be an undigested bit of beef," declared Scrooge to the ghost, "a blot of mustard, a crumb of cheese, a fragment of an underdone potato. There's more of gravy than of the grave about you, whatever you are!"[6] Although this approach to the unconscious acknowledges its existence, it clearly does not take the unconscious very seriously. How valuable can the unconscious be if its manifestation depends on whether one has eaten a pepperoni pizza before bed?

Other approaches grant manifestations of the unconscious mind greater credibility. Sigmund Freud and his disciples believed that neurosis and psychosis originate with experiences that have been intentionally forgotten by the conscious mind because of the trauma and stress associated with them. Although a person may no longer be consciously aware of these "complexes," they still exert their influence on her from the unconscious mind. The purpose of Freudian psychoanalysis, then, is to identify manifestations of the unconscious with traumatic past events and experiences in the life of the patient. By eventually accessing the complexes formed by repressed experiences and releasing them into consciousness, Freudian psychoanalysis enables the patient to confront and overcome them.

Freudian psychology thus assigns great importance to the unconscious mind, but only in a negative way. The unconscious is merely a sinkhole of rotten memories, the "trash can that collects all the refuse of the conscious mind."[7] The unconscious mind is important for Freudian psychoanalysis only because it contains the key to curing mental illness. To the Freudian, the unconscious mind is pathological. The very existence of emanations of unconsciousness into consciousness is evidence of mental illness. The patient becomes cured only when she can release the repressed experiences into the conscious mind. Thus, it is distinctly Freudian to ascribe the voices and visions of ancient prophets to unbalanced hallucination.

Jung and his followers also assigned great importance to the unconscious, but from a much more positive perspective. While Jungians concede that the unconscious mind retains repressed experiences and may sometimes be the source of neurosis or psychosis, they also maintain that manifestations of the unconscious occur as a normal byproduct of life—that is, even among people who are not neurotic. Unconscious images, therefore, are important in their own right. In particular, Jung believed that dreams, visions, and other manifestations of the unconscious mind are important sources of meaning that people can use to interpret and to understand their lives. Jungian psychoanalysis focuses on unconscious images as embodying a message themselves, rather than merely as tools to reach psychological complexes in those who are mentally ill.

Jung once described a patient who had a recurring dream in which a vulgar, drunken, and disheveled woman seemed to be his wife. Since his wife was nothing like this, the patient dismissed the dream as nonsense. A Freudian would have attempted to link the dream with a repressed event or experience by initiating a process of "free association" leading away from the dream. The process would eventually have ended at identifying one or more complexes as the cause of some sort of neurosis in the patient, and the dream that initiated the process would have been forgotten. A Jungian, on the other hand, would have searched for meaning in the dream itself, in an attempt to ascertain what the patient's unconscious mind was attempting to communicate to his consciousness. Jung concluded that the dream signified a conflict in certain ways in which the patient perceived himself to fit in with his surroundings, and especially with women. His conscious mind maintained the fiction that he was a perfect gentleman, when in fact his relatedness to others tended to be vulgar and degenerate.[8]

For the Jungian, then, irruptions of the unconscious mind into consciousness may evidence mental illness, but not necessarily so. The unconscious is a resource for well-adjusted individuals, too. By examining manifestations of their unconscious mind as sources of meaning rather than as symptoms of neurosis, people achieve greater insight into themselves and their lives.

## ARCHETYPES AND THE COLLECTIVE UNCONSCIOUS

Despite the importance of the unconscious mind as a source of personal meaning, for Jung the unconscious had social importance as well. Many of the manifestations of the unconscious mind, he believed, are the result of common psychological attributes of human beings rather than mere individual idiosyncracies. Jung postulated that the human psyche is composed of a collective unconscious as well as a personal one. Just as the human body is the result of millions of years of evolution, so also is the brain. "Our mind has a history," argued Jung, "just as our body has its history. . . . Our unconscious mind, like our body, is a storehouse of relics and memories of the past. A study of the structure of the unconscious collective mind would reveal the same discoveries as you make in comparative anatomy."[9]

The collective unconscious is inherited, just like the general characteristics of the body: "As the body has its basic conformity," maintained Jung, "so has the mind its basic conformity."[10] This idea seems foreign in part because one generally does not think of the mind as having evolved in the sense usually intended by biology. Psychologist Eric Erickson, though not a disciple of Jung, has nevertheless criticized "the semantic assumption that the mind is a 'thing' separate from the body."[11] If the mind is a part of the body, then one might expect it to manifest itself with some consistency through the centuries just as biological phenomena have. This is what Jung believed: "There is no difference in principle between organic and psychic growth. As a plant reproduces its flower, so the psyche creates its symbols."[12]

The symbols of the collective unconscious are collective rather than individual in nature and origin. Whereas the personal unconscious reveals individual psychic patterns, the collective unconscious reveals a psychic pattern common to all humans. Jung labeled these common patterns "archetypes." They are the manifestation of general psychic forms that assert themselves in similar ways regardless of cultural or personal context. Jung sometimes referred to them as the unconscious images of biological instincts and suggested that, like instincts, the archetypes are both innate and inherited.

Jung maintained throughout his life that the existence of the collective unconscious could be verified empirically, by analyzing the dreams, visions, and other irruptions of the unconscious mind into conscious experience, and then controlling for personal and cultural variations. After excluding all motifs that might possibly be known to a dreamer, any remaining motifs that function consistently across individuals and cultures are manifestations of the collective unconscious—the archetypes.[13] As an example, Jung tells the story of a patient who was suffering from paranoid schizophrenia:

> One day I came across [this patient], blinking through the window up at the sun, and moving his head from side to side in a curious manner. He took me by the arm and said he wanted to show me something. He said I must look at the sun with eyes half shut, and then I could see the sun's phallus. If I moved my head from side to side the sun-phallus would move too, and that was the origin of the wind.[14]

This occurred in 1906. Jung later came across a Greek myth, first translated in 1910, which described the source of the wind to be a tube hanging from the sun. Further research yielded numerous classical and medieval variations on the same image. Jung ruled out the possibility that the patient, an ordinary consulate clerk in his early twenties, had been exposed to the myth and later forgotten it—he did not know Greek and had little education. From this Jung concluded that the image was archetypal, an idea that is not intellectually inherited from others, but rather one that has always existed in the human psyche and that can be found again and again in the most diverse minds in all periods of history.[15]

Although the idea of the collective unconscious remains controversial, it has been highly influential. Freud himself conceded the existence of "archaic remnants—mental forms whose presence cannot be explained by anything in the individual's own life and which seem to be aboriginal, innate, and inherited shapes of the human mind."[16] The idea is particularly influential among non-Freudians who interpret manifestations of the unconscious as potential reservoirs of personal meaning rather than unavoidable evidence of mental disease. American mythologist Joseph Campbell went so far as to proclaim that the "truth" of the existence of the collective unconscious is "beyond question" in the literature of psychology.[17]

It is important to understand that an archetype is not an "unconscious idea"; indeed, it is not defined by reference to its content at all. Archetypes do not consist of the images that are stimulated in the conscious mind by the structures of the unconscious mind; such images are only representations of the archeypes. Thus, dreams are not archetypes, but merely their image. Jung himself asserted that it was ridiculous to think that a particular representation of an archetype could be inherited. An archetype is infused with the definition and content of a particular image or motif only after it manifests itself in the conscious mind and is filled up with cultural ballast.

Rather than the particular representation, the archetype is the psychic tendency to form such representations in the first place, irrespective of their content. Thus, the archetype is not substantive, but form that attracts substance; rather than meaning, the archetype is antecedent to meaning. It is a verb rather than a noun. Religious historian Mircea Eliade once observed that myth is "produced" by the archetypes in the same way that Gustave Flaubert's 19th century classic on infidelity, *Madame Bovary*, was "produced" by adultery.[18] Just as the persistence of adultery within the repressed confines of Victorian mores demanded an explanation, so also the demands of the archetypes upon the psyche stimulate the formulation of explanations which satisfy those demands. One might call the archetypes, then, "psychological imperatives." They are deep psychological needs that powerfully call forth efforts to satisfy them.

For example, the concept of the "second birth" is an archetypal image that is found in virtually every culture in the world. It reassures "that death is not final, that it is always followed by new birth."[19] This idea is closely related to the archetype of the "hero" or "rescuer," who overcomes destruction and preserves or restores whatever was threatened, usually at the cost of the hero's own life. Clearly Christ the Redeemer is an archetypal image, since Christians believe that Jesus overcame death and sin on the cross, thereby granting resurrection and eternal life to all believers. The second birth archetype is also present in premodern initiation rituals, whereby adolescents symbolically "die," only to emerge "reborn" as full-fledged adults. Again, the nearly identical image is present in Christianity in the ritual of baptism, by which the believer lays aside her "old life" and is newly born in the faith.

Paul the Apostle wrote in the New Testament: "We died to sin: how can we live in it any longer? Have you forgotten that when we were baptized into union with Christ Jesus we were baptized into his death? By baptism we were buried with him, and lay dead, in order that, as Christ was raised from the dead in the splendour of the Father, so also we might set our feet upon the new path of life."[20] Thus, although the archetype is the universal fear of non-existence or stagnation, its cultural image may take many forms. Other archetypal images include the divine king or good shepherd, the ascent to great heights, and the narrow passage or bridge to a better world.

It is not inevitable, of course, that archetypal images be religious, at least not in contemporary life. One explanation of the power of Marxist thought in the 20th century—only recently diluted—is that it depicted archetypal images that appeared to satisfy the needs of the collective unconscious in the same way that religion does.[21] One of the major themes of Marxism, wrote Jung, was "the time-hallowed archetypal dream of a Golden Age (or Paradise), where everything is provided in abundance for everyone, and a great, just, and wise chief rules over a human kindergarten."[22]

Jung believed, however, that most of the archetypes manifested themselves religiously. In premodern or religious societies archetypal images are typically religious as well. In a country like the United States, then, where until recently culture had been implicitly Protestant and where large numbers of people still profess both belief in God and commitment to organized religion, it is not surprising that the most potent and frequently manifested cultural symbols, those that satisfy or provoke the collective unconscious, have deep religious significance.

## UNCONSCIOUSNESS AND BELIEF IN MODERN SOCIETY

As we discussed in Chapter 3, since the 1930s public culture in the United States has largely been shaped by science. In contemporary American society, there is a clear bias for ways of knowing that are empirically verifiable. Those who purport to describe reality through intuition, dreams, and other manifestations of the unconscious are at a severe disadvantage against those who can marshall the power of scientific experimentation and method to support their conclusions. Unconscious manifestations in normal people are a threatening challenge to the scientific mind, since they cannot be accounted for by logic and observation. Hence the historical preference for Freud over Jung in characterizing the unconscious. History since the Enlightenment records a sustained modernist assault upon superstition and myth, with the most powerful attack focused upon traditional beliefs in God and religion. The general inhospitability of public culture both to religious experiences and to unconscious experiences in general bears testimony to the power of rationalism and empiricism in contemporary American life.

This bias toward rationalism and empiricism blocks one from acquiring unconscious knowledge, and dissociates her from the rich and meaningful symbols that originate in the unconscious mind. "Logical analysis is the prerogative of consciousness," wrote Jung, "we select with reason and knowledge."[23] Without the unconscious, humanity is left with a sterile rationality that is fearful and repressive of phenomena that cannot be understood and explained by reference to ordinary conscious experience. Moreover, the unconscious mind in general and the archetypes in particular usually manifest themselves in a religious context. As the Christian cross dramatically illustrates, much of religious experience depends on symbols that are rooted in the unconscious. Thus, the hostility of the scientific age to manifestations of the unconscious mind is merely the general example of the more specific hostility of public culture to religious experience.

Regardless of whether religious experiences are scientifically demonstrable, large numbers of Americans rely on the symbols of such experiences to give greater meaning to their lives—meaning that cannot be drawn from consciousness alone. In a society that devalues and ignores manifestations of the unconscious mind, including religious experiences, the religious person is fragmented. She stands in danger of losing the ability to relate to her unconscious mind, and thus to her total being. Because the power of religious symbols derives in part from their link to the archetypes in the unconscious mind, they are difficult, and perhaps impossible, to discard even when one wishes to.

An archetype persists in manifesting itself through cultural symbols irrespective of humanity's attempts to understand and control it. If an archetype is indeed like a biological instinct, as Jung argued, then just as biological instincts are necessary for physical survival, archetypes are essential for psychological survival. In other words, the cultural symbols that are spawned by the archetypes represent and satisfy a psychological need that humans generally must meet in order to survive.

Consider, for example, the vast and complex symbols and cultures, including virtually all of the major world religious movements, that have been built around the attempt to understand and control life and death. We referred to some of these in discussing the archetypal image of rebirth. Like the archetypes of which it is a manifestation, religious worship—the acknowledgement of transcendent persons and entities who have power over humans and their lives—has always been part of history. To eliminate or ignore religion, then, is to attempt to eliminate or ignore one of the most widespread methods of satisfying the psychological need to know and understand the meaning of one's existence.

We realize that many religious people are not flattered by the idea that their faith is psychologically generated. Indeed, we sympathize with this reaction to a significant extent, as will become clear in Chapter 7. Nevertheless, the relation of religious belief to the unconscious mind is an important one that must be understood for one to appreciate, from a secular standpoint, the pressure that public secularism exerts on religious people, and the potentially explosive consequences that such pressure could trigger. The possibility that religion is a manifestation of a psychological archetype has critically important implications for the role of religion in contemporary public life.

First, if Jung's postulation of the collective unconscious is valid, then by banning from public life the archetypal symbols of religion, one interferes with a fundamental, necessary part of human existence. If accomplished with severity and longevity, the privatization of religion threatens to dehumanize the large number of Americans who have dealt with the archetypes by religious worship. The principal means of satisfying their psychological demands simply vanishes from the cultural radar screen. The secularization of public life is not only consciously oppressive and alienating, but unconsciously so as well, by its exclusion of basic structures of human psychological existence.

Second, and even more important, since religion is the manifestation of one or more psychological archetypes, it will not gently fade away like an old soldier just because public culture ignores it. Archetypes are so essentially part of human psychology that no degree of blocking or control can repress them. One way or another, archetypes will always circumvent attempts to suppress them.

The anger and force with which some religious individuals and groups in the United States have reacted to public secularization and religious privatization, then, is at least partially attributable to the demands of the collective unconscious. Such alienation is the natural result of attempts to suppress the psychological demands of the archetypes. This hones a sharper, edge to our suggestion that the alienation of religious believers carries the potential for revolution. Jung himself suggested that revolution under these conditions is especially violent and uncontrolled.[24] The deep need to preserve the meaning that is poured into the psychological demands of the collective unconscious is driven by forces that are both primal and beyond conscious control.

## NOTES

1. Carl G. Jung, "Approaching the Unconscious" in *Man and His Symbols*, ed. Carl G. Jung (New York: Dell, 1968), 24.

2. Ibid., 27.

3. Ibid., 82.

4. Quoted in Alfred Hock, *Reason and Genius: A Study in Origins* (New York: Philosophical Library, 1960), 66–67.

5. See Bertrand Russell, *Religion and Science* (New York: Oxford University Press, 1961), 113–14.

6. Charles Dickens, *A Christmas Carol* (New York: Macmillan, 1937), 27–28.

7. Quoted in Jung, "Approaching the Unconscious," 32.

8. Ibid., 14–17.

9. Carl G. Jung, *Analytical Psychology: Its Theory and Practice*, 1st Amendment ed. (New York: Pantheon, 1968), 44, 45.

10. Ibid., 46.

11. Erik H. Erikson, *Childhood and Society*, 2d ed. (New York: Norton, 1963), 23.

12. Jung, "Approaching the Unconscious," 53.

13. Jung, *Analytical Psychology*, 44.

14. Carl G. Jung, "The Structure of the Psyche" in *The Portable Jung*, ed. Joseph Campbell, trans. Ronald Hull (New York: Penguin, 1976), 36.

15. Ibid., 36–37.

16. Quoted in Jung, "Approaching the Unconscious," 57.

17. Joseph Campbell, "Mythological Themes in Creative Literature and Art" in *Myths, Dreams, and Religion*, ed. Joseph Campbell (New York: Dutton, 1970), 170.

18. Mircea Eliade, *The Sacred and the Profane: The Nature of Religion*, trans. Willard R. Trask (New York: Harcourt Brace Jovanovich, 1959), 209–210.

19. Ibid., 156.

20. Romans 6.2–4 (New English Bible).

21. E.g., Eliade, *The Sacred and the Profane*, 204–10.

22. Jung, "Approaching the Unconscious," 73–74.

23. Ibid., 67.

24. Jung, *Analytical Psychology*, 50.

# Chapter 5

# Religion and the Rational

The secularism that has come to dominate American public life unavoidably results in the defamation and devaluation of religious belief, because religious belief by its nature entails strong elements that cannot be rationally or empirically accounted for. This conflict between the secularism of public life and the beliefs that inform the private lives of religious Americans creates an oppressive tension. On the one hand, religious Americans are pressured either to dilute or to abandon their beliefs; and on the other hand, they feel pressure from their religious beliefs to reject the institutions and processes of public life and subordinate rationality and empiricism to those beliefs.

The secularism of public life thus excludes the person who has religious experiences. These experiences tend to be intuitive and spiritual. Almost by definition, religious experiences are not rational and not empirical, as modern society has come to understand those terms. Public culture thus discounts religious experiences, because they cannot be rationally explained or empirically demonstrated. When religious experiences are positive in a person's life, their devaluation by society erects a barrier between society and those who have had such experiences. The religious individual knows firsthand that her religious experiences are good, but also knows that society considers those who have had such experiences eccentric at best, and perhaps even dangerous.

Whenever the religious person participates in public life, she must choose between her religious experiences and the rational and empirical modes of public life. This conflict generates deep conflicts in religious people. Each time they choose to rely on their religious experiences, they distance themselves from the norms of American public life. Yet each time they choose the norms of public life, they distance themselves from those experiences that have the greatest personal meaning.

## THE ANTIPATHY OF MODERNISM TO RELIGION

The implicit assumption of contemporary public culture in the United States is that God, if he exists at all, does not talk to us and never did. Figures in history who purported to be acting on knowledge received from a transcendent or divine source are usually considered abnormal, affected by some pathological mental disorder which caused them to behave irrationally. In this view, Joan of Arc, for example, did not really hear the voices of the saints, but suffered from mental delusions which made her mistake her own thoughts for divine revelation.

To be sure, sometimes the explanation is utilized without the negative implication that religious experience is the result of mental illness. Psychologist Julian Jaynes, for example, has argued that the "unicameral" or unified mind is a relatively recent phenomenon. As recently as several thousand years ago, according to Jaynes, the mental processes of the two halves of the brain were not integrated. Thus, functions of the left brain were perceived by the right brain as phenomena and stimuli external to the mind, and vice versa. Jaynes uses this theory of the ancient "bicameral mind" to interpret the purportedly divine revelations recorded by Old Testament prophets as naive mental impressions at a time when mental processes were not fully integrated. God was not talking to humanity; rather, the left brain was merely talking to the right.[1]

Whether the secular explanation of religious experience is pathological or developmental, its thrust is the same: Religious experience is not an encounter with transcendent reality, but merely (and wholly) a manifestation of human biology and psychology. (The discussion of Jungian archetypes in chapter 4, as important as it is in understanding the powerful hold that religion has on people, is subject to the same criticism.) The often substantial followings of historical prophet figures is attributed to charisma and demagoguery, rather than to the spirituality or truth of the doctrines they preached. Indeed, the possibility that the claimed religious experiences of these prophets might actually have happened is not seriously considered. Twentieth-century humanity, after all, is thought to have outgrown the need for fairy tales like God. We now live in a brave new scientific world in which people rely on their own powers of reasoning and empirical discovery to determine what is "real" about the world. Through the scientific method, we believe we can "discover, by means of observation and reasoning based upon it, particular facts about the world. . . ."[2]

This bias towards science survives in the study and practice of law. Legal reasoning had formerly been thought of as a rational and logical process by which one discovers the necessary limits on human behavior that must be observed for peaceful social coexistence. Lawyers and judges believed that the study of legal precedents illuminates unique solutions to legal disputes. Christopher Columbus Langdell, one-time dean of the Harvard Law School and the father of modern legal education, believed that law was a science all of whose materials could be found in books.[3]

Few lawyers believe in such a simplistic view of law these days, but the scientific interpretation of law continues to have its effect. To this day, the legal process remains focused on objective and empirical inquiry. This preoccupation with determinacy and objectivity makes it difficult for law to account for religious experience. The essence of religious belief is personal spiritual experience that can be communicated to others, if at all, only with great difficulty, unless they are part of the same community of belief. The process by which one develops belief in a transcendent reality—acquires faith—is not and cannot be a wholly rational or empirical process. Although reason and logic play a part in religious conversion and belief, ultimately the validity of one's faith cannot be observed, measured, tested, or otherwise proved (or disproved) by accepted scientific methods. In the end, religious experience must be taken "on faith."

Thus, when the law must deal with religious experience, it uses a language and a process habituated to objectivity, rationality, and empiricism to describe and evaluate experiences which at their root are subjective, nonrational, and unobservable. The touchstones of religious experience—faith, belief, and revelation—are foreign to the legal system. It is inevitable, then, that law will systematically devalue religious experience. Legal language and process are currently incapable of capturing and conveying the essence of that experience.

## CONSTITUTIONAL LAW AND NATIVE AMERICAN RELIGION

The rationalistic and empirical biases of the legal system are clearly evident in the way in which the courts have treated native American religious claims. In general, these actions challenge government land-use policies which native Americans believe are incompatible with the practice of their tribal religions. Several judicial decisions illustrate the problem. In the case of *Wilson v. Block*,[4] for example, the Hopi and Navajo tribes challenged a decision by the United States Forest Service to permit the expansion of a ski resort located on federally owned, nontribal land in the San Francisco Peaks of northern Arizona.

The Navajos believe that the Peaks are one of four sacred mountains that are home to specific Navajo deities, and that the Peaks themselves are a living deity. They also believe that special healing powers inhere in the Peaks which would be impaired by the contemplated expansion. The Hopis believe that the "Kachinas"—special emissaries of the Hopi Creator which protect and sustain Hopi villages—reside at the Peaks part of each year, and that the expansion would directly insult the Kachinas and the Creator. The tribes argued, among other things, that the contemplated expansion would deny them the access to the Peaks necessary to perform their religious ceremonies and further, that the expansion would constitute a sacrilegious desecration of the central objects of worship of their respective faiths.

Not surprisingly, the court responded eagerly to the first argument about access. The utilitarian calculus—ascertaining the most socially desirable balance or resolution of a conflict between opposing interests— is what courts do most, and what they think they do best. Because only 777 of the 75,000 acres of the Peaks were proposed to be developed, and because the tribes would retain access even to those 777 acres, the court had little difficulty finding that native American religious *practices* would not be significantly impaired by the contemplated expansion. Accordingly, infringement upon the native Americans' religious practices—their "free exercise of religion"—was found insufficient by the court to justify blocking the proposed expansion.

The court had considerably more difficulty with the second argument. The essence of this argument is that the governmentally-approved sacrilege represented by the contemplated expansion would publicly and officially defame and devalue the tribal religions. The likely result, as the Hopi tribal chairman testified, will be the destruction of tribal religious culture:

It is my opinion that in the long run if the expansion is permitted, we will not be able successfully to teach our people that this is a sacred place. If the ski resort remains or is expanded, our people will not accept the view that this is the sacred home of the Kachinas. The basis of our existence as a society will become a mere fairy tale to our people. If our people no longer possess this long held belief and way of life, which will inevitably occur with the continued presence of the ski resort, . . . a direct and negative impact on our religious practices [will result]. The destruction of these practices will also destroy our present way of life and culture.[5]

What does one do in the 20th century with a people who sincerely believe that a mountain is a God, or the sacred home of Gods? Taking these beliefs seriously requires that one admit the possibility that the Peaks are "alive," or that the Kachinas really do visit them every year. These propositions sound ridiculous to the modern mind even when advanced as mere possibilities. A judge who took them seriously would risk considerable embarrassment. (One wonders in this connection how the central Christian narrative of crucifixion and resurrection must have sounded to 1st century Romans.)

Majority or well-known religions escape this to a large extent, since their familiarity makes even their most fantastic theological claims seem unsurprising, if perhaps a bit silly. Minority religions like those of native Americans, however, are tinged with a bizarre and ridiculous hue. By contrast, a ski resort is something familiar that one can see and analyze. Most important, the resort is something whose economic value can be calculated with some precision on the basis of projected revenues and alternative uses. Thus, the resolution of the conflict in *Wilson v. Block* was decisively influenced by the rationality and empiricism that is embedded in the legal system—one cannot be surprised that what the majority culture commonly understands and measures (the resort) prevailed over what it does not understand and cannot measure (native American religion).

The Supreme Court itself has devalued native American religious practices in much the same way and, one suspects, for much the same reasons. In one recent decision in this area, *Lyng v. Northwest Indian Cemetery Protective Association*,[6] the Court considered a native American challenge to a government-sponsored road construction plan on federally owned, nontribal land. The land adjacent to the planned logging road, however, was conceded by all sides to be integrally related to certain native American religious practices. In particular, the affected tribes contended that the road would remove the privacy, silence, and undisturbed natural setting of the area, all of which are critically necessary to their religious practice.

Despite its admission that construction of the road "could have devastating effects on traditional Indian religious practices,"[7] the Court refused to halt construction, on the theory that the land belonged to the government and it therefore could do what it wished with it. The Court rather clearly indicated its lack of commitment to free exercise of native American religion when it conceded that it would not grant the tribes' relief even if construction of the road would "virtually destroy the Indians' ability to practice their religion."[8] Roads can be seen, and their economic utility measured. The sanctity of religious worship is unseen and without measure; it is, therefore, without protection.

These decisions are representative of the legal system's treatment of native American religious belief and practice. In recent years, virtually every native American religious challenge to federal land-use regulations has failed.[9] In general, the only native American religious challenges to government that have succeeded are those in which granting the challenge has little or no economic cost—that is, those in which the importance of the government's regulatory interest was so doubtful that the difficulty of measuring the value of native American religious beliefs became unimportant. Thus, a court was willing to set aside the conviction of a native American for killing a single moose out of season for use in a tribal funeral ceremony.[10] Similarly, courts have approved the use of the illegal drug peyote in the bona fide religious ceremonies of remote desert tribes.[11] (A recent decision of the Supreme Court involving native Americans, however, has placed these decisions in jeopardy.[12]) However, when protecting religious belief and practice costs money, as it always does in land-use challenges, the legal system can rarely bring itself to recognize the seriousness of native American religious claims.

We emphasize that our point is not that native American religious claims (or anyone else's) obviously should prevail whenever they conflict with government objectives; societal objectives might reasonably be thought to outweigh even religious liberty. However, if this is the test, then surely a tribe's proof that particular government action will lead to the extinction of its religion should be weighted very heavily against the economic or social need asserted by the government. In such cases, the government should be expected to identify a particularly important justification for its actions. It would certainly be reasonable to conclude that the threat of religious extinction is outweighed by, for example, a life-or-death threat to other members of society presented by a particular religious practice. Religiously motivated human sacrifice is an obvious, if exaggerated, example.[13]

More realistically, courts have typically upheld general prohibitions on the possession and transportation of poisonous snakes even against religious snake handlers.[14] Similarly, courts have generally refused to allow parents to withhold vaccinations, inoculations, and medical treatment from their children on religious grounds (although adults usually can refuse treatment for themselves).[15] By contrast, a decision to risk destruction of tribal religious culture for the sake of a ski resort, as in *Wilson*, or a logging road, as in *Lyng*, is problematic at best.

## CONSTITUTIONAL LAW AND (NON)PROTECTION OF RELIGION

Native Americans are perhaps most vulnerable to insensitivity on the part of government because their beliefs are not widely known or understood. Native American beliefs are thus particularly jarring to the sensibilities of the majority. Native Americans are far from the only religious Americans, however, who suffer at the hands of a rationalist and empiricist legal culture. The callous treatment of native American religious beliefs is only a particular example of the general devaluation that religion receives in the legal system.

Americans are proud that their Constitution affirmatively protects religious liberty—the "free exercise of religion." In fact, however, the existence of the free exercise clause has made virtually no difference to religious liberty in the United States. In most cases, the Supreme Court has interpreted the clause to permit substantial infringement of religious liberty by government.

The free exercise clause did not prevent relentless federal persecution of Mormon polygamists that nearly destroyed the Mormon church in the late 19th century.[16] It did not protect orthodox Jewish merchants, who close their businesses on Saturday to observe their sabbath, from economic loss when Sunday closing laws forced them to close on the Christian sabbath as well.[17] The free exercise clause did not protect Bob Jones University from losing its federal tax exemption when the Internal Revenue Service deemed the University's racially discriminatory theology contrary to public policy.[18] It did not protect the Amish from payment of social security taxes in violation of their religion, even though they agreed to provide for their own retirements and not to seek benefits.[19] The free exercise clause did not protect the military career of a Jew who wore a yarmulke in violation of uniform regulations.[20] And most recently, it did not prevent two native Americans from being denied state unemployment benefits when they were fired for having ingested peyote as part of a sacred religious ritual.[21]

The Supreme Court has protected religious liberty in only two kinds of cases. First, as the native American cases suggest, it will protect religious liberty when the social cost of doing so is very low. For example, if a person is fired for refusing to work on her religious sabbath, the state may not deny her unemployment compensation.[22] Now, unemployment benefits in this situation are nice, but a deep commitment to religious liberty would prevent firings for sabbath observance in the first place. This, however, the Court has declined to do.[23] The cost of accommodating the varieties of sabbath observance in the United States is just too high.

Similarly, the Court has held that the Old Order Amish, who fear the moral corrosion of secular public education, need not send their children to school after the 8th grade despite a state law which requires attendance through the 10th grade.[24] The Court wrote its opinion in this case so narrowly that lower courts have interpreted it to create a religious exemption only for the Amish. After all, if large numbers of Americans sought religious exemptions from school attendance, public school systems would be severely disrupted. Thus, fundamentalist Christians have been denied exemptions from public school reading programs, even though many of the books that their children are required to read insult, offend, and undermine their religious beliefs.[25]

The second group of cases involve situations in which the religious practice at issue can be analyzed as part of a larger, secular category of constitutional protection. For example, the Supreme Court declared unconstitutional a municipal ordinance that prevented Jehovah's Witnesses from distributing religious pamphlets. The Witnesses believe that they are under a divine obligation to testify of their beliefs to the world. However, the Court did not invalidate the ordinance because it violated the free exercise of religion, but rather because it violated the freedom of speech.[26]

The Court apparently is willing to protect religious exercise in cases like this, but not because the conduct is *religious*. Protection is forthcoming only because the religious conduct looks like *nonreligious* conduct that is protected by another constitutional provision.[27] This, of course, makes the free exercise clause largely redundant. Why do we need a separate clause protecting the free exercise of religion when the protection it affords is no broader than what is available under the freedom of speech clause?

Law professor Mark Tushnet has summarized the Supreme Court's doctrine in this area as protecting religious liberty only to the extent that either (i) the religious practice in question can be reduced to a secular constitutional right, like freedom of speech; or (ii) protecting the practice will encroach only marginally upon the goals and interests of secular society.[28] This lukewarm protection of religious liberty, such as it is, is probably better than no protection at all. Nevertheless, Americans should not fool themselves into thinking that religious liberty is significantly protected by the Constitution. The Supreme Court has made it clear that it will protect religious liberty only when the cost of doing so is trivial.

## THE REACTIONS OF RELIGION TO MODERNISM

Just as the failure to protect native American religious practices is characteristic of a general devaluation of religion by the legal system, so also this cavalier treatment of religion by the legal system is characteristic of a general devaluation of religion throughout American public life. As we discussed earlier, American public culture does not admit the possibility that God—or any transcendent reality—truly exists. Belief in God is viewed by participants in public life as the refuge of those too insecure to stand on their own. Public culture will tolerate religious belief, however, on certain conditions. One of these conditions is that the God believed in be a relatively remote one who intervenes in human affairs only when an alternative rational explanation is available. Thus, one may publicly thank God for the blessing of rain that ends a drought, so long as cloud-seeding has been proceeding apace. The assertion that God is the sole cause of a course of events, however, is clearly out of bounds. It is acceptable to make vague references to prayer and the Almighty at a presidential inaugural. However, the president who admits that he regularly prays for guidance in making national decisions, and acts on his inspiration, is likely to make many people very nervous.

Similarly, public culture is accustomed to people who credit God for having helped them survive life-threatening accidents or illnesses. Those who insist, however, that it really *was* God (and not the surgeon) who pulled them through are thought to be a little off-center. From the perspective of the cultural elite, religious people, regardless of their actual numbers, constitute in sociologist Peter Berger's words a "cognitive minority" in public life. Berger defines a cognitive minority as "a group of people whose view of the world differs significantly from the one generally taken for granted in their society . . . , a group formed around a body of deviant 'knowledge.' "[29]

In American public life, serious belief in the divine or transcendent is unquestionably deviant. Thus, when someone like Pat Robertson baldly asserts that the power of prayer can avert natural calamities and heal deadly illnesses, he is subjected to withering criticism and ridicule. (Since it seems that Robertson was pandering to fundamentalist Republicans when he declared this, some criticism was probably deserved, although not the criticism he actually received. The criticism should not have been directed at his belief in the possibility that God can be called through prayer to intervene in human affairs, but rather at his cynical attempt to use that belief to political advantage.) God is accepted as a remnant of days gone by, but not as a major actor in contemporary events. As we recounted earlier, those who shape and report on public life tend to filter God and religion out of any position of importance or influence.

Yet many Americans still strongly believe in the relevance of religion to contemporary life; Pat Robertson is not the only American left who believes in the power of prayer, and this belief is not merely abstract and theoretical. Many religious Americans have experienced what they take to be God's personal intervention in their lives, and many of these can powerfully recount more than one such experience. It is clearly the case in the United States that many of its inhabitants believe that they have personally experienced divine manifestations in their lives. How are they to react when public culture ignores, criticizes, or ridicules experiences that they hold both real and sacred?

## Domesticated Religion

When religious people find themselves and their religious experiences—their most sacred and meaningful experiences—treated as eccentric, irrelevant, and even dangerous, they experience conflicting feelings. An immediate and understandable reaction is some defensiveness and embarrassment. Religious people are not ignorant; they understand better than most the difficult conflict between religious belief and the rationalism and empiricism of modern life, because they must live it.

One strategy for dealing with this conflict is to confine the religious and the secular aspects of one's life to different social spheres. Extra-rational religious experiences can be deemphasized and described in rational language in public contexts, with their fullest and richest religious meaning spoken only in private. For example, the Navajos and the Hopis, if they chose, could avoid ridicule for their anachronistic religious beliefs by describing them more as cultural, sociological phenomena—"mythic" stories that preserve tribal "heritage," rather than literal descriptions of reality. "Myths" and "heritage" are words that public culture can understand; they signal that the tribes do not take their religion all that seriously, and can be dealt with as moderns like the rest of the United States. Religious people who choose this strategy thus aid and abet the presumption of privatized religion urged by public culture.

Moreover, whether a religious person who is truly a believer can succeed for any significant length of time in pursuing such a strategy of dilution is doubtful. The religious person who successfully compartmentalizes her religious beliefs and experiences by disguising or abandoning them in public contexts precipitates an existential crisis. Religion constructs reality and creates cosmological meaning for the believer; it is the necessary prerequisite to her being. "There can be no knowledge of God," writes law professor Milner Ball, "apart from his revelation of himself."[30] Similarly, theologian Stanley Hauerwas argues that Christians cannot coherently discuss what their religious beliefs demand in the way of proper living without reference to the life, death, and resurrection of Jesus.[31] To the religious person, to disguise one's religious beliefs is to disguise the meaning of one's existence; abandonment of the sacred means abandonment of being itself. Law professor Michael Perry has written that

one can participate in politics and law . . . only as a partisan of particular moral/religious convictions. . . . One's basic moral/religious convictions are (partly) self-constitutive and are therefore a principal ground—indeed, the principal ground—of political deliberation. To "bracket" such convictions is therefore to bracket—to annihilate—essential aspects of one's very self.[32]

Perry argues that since religious convictions are a large part of what makes a religious person the unique personality that she is, that person can authentically participate in public life only as a *religious* person. If she attempts to participate with her religious beliefs masked or disguised, she is not participating as the person she really is, but as "some one—or some thing—else."[33] Similarly, Kent Greenawalt has noted the unfairness and absurdity of asking religious people to keep their convictions under wraps when participating in public life: "To demand that many devout Catholics, Protestants, and Jews pluck out their religious convictions is to ask them how they would think about a critical moral problem if they started from scratch, disregarding what they presently take as basic premises of moral thought."[34] For the Navajos and the Hopis, then, to abandon the Creator and the Kachinas as cosmic realities, even if just in a public context, is unthinkable. It would require that they abandon in that context the single framework that gives each tribe—and each tribal member—a unique identity in the universe.

To the person whose religion demands integration of faith with life, whose religious belief creates her sense of place in the cosmos, abandoning the sacred in any portion of her life, even temporarily or superficially, creates oppressive tensions. Psychology suggests that an internal conflict this severe and this deep cannot persist for long in any individual. Indeed, Jungian psychology suggests that compartmentalization requires the impossibility of ignoring or suppressing the demands of the archetypes. Under the theory of cognitive dissonance, this kind of conflict is believed to result from a person's having made a decision that contradicts reliable, widely believed information that also is accepted by the decisionmaker. The decisionmaker experiences a conscious effect of psychological pressure or dislocation known as "dissonance." Dissonance results from having made a decision that is inconsistent with conventional wisdom about how the world works. Thus, a decision to credit extra-rational religious experiences by a person who regularly functions in the rational world creates dissonance. Dissonance is uncomfortable, because most people require some degree of external approval and reinforcement of their self-concept as a matter of psychological health. Mythologist Joseph Campbell has observed that throughout history, visionaries, leaders, and heroes have always been close to neurotic, because they attempt to act out dreams and visions that have never been experienced by the "normal" world, and thereby live in a fearful and lonely world of unmediated, uninterpreted "original experience".[35]

In sum, because most humans find it easier to maintain a self-concept that is more or less consistent with their perception of the social environment in which they live, the common human response to dissonance is to seek to reduce or to eliminate it.[36] If one's religious beliefs are judged implausible by the larger society in which she lives, then the vitality and relevance of those beliefs are at risk, Peter Berger writes, "not just in our dealings with others, but much more importantly in our own minds."[37] In the words of James Boyd White, "one cannot maintain forever one's language and judgment and feelings against the pressure of a world that works in different ways, for one is in some measure the product of that world."[38]

Dissonance theory, then, suggests that after a decision to become or to remain committed to religious experiences or beliefs, believers will experience dissonance stemming from the secularism that pervades American public life and that sharply contrasts with their religious faith. The theory further suggests that believers will attempt to eliminate the dissonance by moving to modify aspects of one or both of the conflicting positions so that they become compatible. The starkest, most extreme choice presented to the religious believer who is unsuccessful at compartmentalizing the religious and the secular aspects of her existence is to choose between the two; either by abandoning her faith, or by subordinating rationality to faith as the more reliable way of living.

As we have argued, simply abandoning one's faith precipitates the existential crisis in its most potent form. What one wants in this circumstance is elimination of the tension between the demands of secularism and those of religious belief, without feeling that one has abandoned the cosmic structure of reality that is created by religious belief. One way to accomplish this is to avoid asserting religiously based claims in public contexts whenever possible, and instead to conform the demands of religious belief to the policy prescriptions of one or more legitimate—that is to say secular—public agendas. Thus, without wholly abandoning her religion, one publicly mutes it and endorses a compatible secular political agenda. One does this, however, not because her religious beliefs *necessarily* demand the agenda or even coincide with it, but because agreement with the secular agenda reduces feelings of dissonance and alienation from public life.

Richard Neuhaus has accused the mainline Protestant churches of marginalizing themselves in precisely this way by essentially aligning themselves with the left wing of the Democratic Party.[39] One might also characterize the religious right as having done the same thing with respect to the Republican Party, although it is probably more accurate to describe that party as having bent to the fundamentalists, rather than vice versa. Eventually, acquiescing to its banishment from public life, and saying little to distinguish itself from secular interest groups, religion becomes tamed and domesticated. This kind of religion is neutered. It has "little to say other than what the world wants to hear."[40] It does not pervade the lives of its believers and command their allegiance, and it is unlikely to move them to action.

This neutralization of religion is a serious development in a country like the United States, where religious people and organizations have always been publicly and politically engaged. Sociologist Robert Bellah has argued that efforts to develop the American consciousness of individual freedom and autonomy in the 19th century would have been ineffective without parallel reinforcement by Protestant revivalism.[41] It remains an open question whether purely secular belief systems can command the same respect from Americans that religion does. Yet ultimately, domesticated religion is distinguishable from secularism itself only by decorative trimmings of prayer and piety at the edges of fundamentally secular arguments. The only virtue (if one can call it that) of domesticated religion is that it preserves institutional forms of worship and belief, so that the existential crisis seems to be avoided.

### Radicalized Religion

While one response to the tension between secular public life and religious private life (short of abandoning religious belief altogether) is to dilute religious belief in public contexts without altogether abandoning it, another response is to subordinate secularism to religious belief. Many religious Americans have chosen not to circumscribe and dilute their religious beliefs as the means of dealing with the secularization of public life. On the contrary, many seem to defy that secularization, at least in certain spheres of public life. The ban on public school prayer by the Supreme Court remains controversial despite the passage of time; more than 20 years later, 80 percent of the population supports prayer in the public schools, while only 10 percent support the Court's decisions in this area.[42] In fact, while most Americans support the general principle of church–state separation, large numbers dissent from the rigor with which the Supreme Court has applied the principle.[43]

This defiance of public secularism has manifested itself in other ways. The religious right premises its public policy positions with declarations of sectarian beliefs which it holds valid for everyone, believer or not. A believer who is both faithful to her own tradition and sensitive to the diversity of belief in the United States might preface religiously based public policy arguments with something like, "For Catholics . . ." or "If one is Christian. . . ." The religious right articulates no such premise. It interprets history and current events by the idiosyncratic light of its own fundamentalist lamp, and nevertheless insists that its interpretations are controlling for everyone.[44]

It is not enough that the Supreme Court and other custodians of public life have in their wisdom determined that a secular public life is constitutionally required or socially desirable. Such unilateral declarations only heighten the potential for alienation by suggesting that secularism is being imposed by an unelected elite that is far from a political majority. People who have been socialized in a system where the "majority rules" may accept a political loss suffered "fair and square" in the political marketplace of democracy. By contrast, they often become resentful and angry at having been deprived of the opportunity for political victory by politically unaccountable elements of the government, such as the courts and administrative agencies. Some of the angry fervor of pro-life activists, for example, undoubtedly stems from their perception that the Supreme Court unfairly preempted their political position by constitutionalizing a woman's right to have an abortion and thereby placing regulation of access to abortions largely beyond the reach of legislative politics.

A secularized public culture eventually forces religious people to choose whether to modify their beliefs to gain the respect of public culture, or instead to subordinate the secular knowledge of public life to their religious beliefs and risk ignorance or ridicule by nonbelievers. The pressure of this choice will result either in abandonment of religion or in its alienation from public life. As we have argued, American democracy is critically dependent on the support of its people for the underlying political system. Thus, the secularization of public life, if it does not trivialize religion, results in disaffection with and disobedience of majoritarian norms and values. "We have seen," wrote theologian Reinhold Niebuhr, referring to 1920s bootleggers and 1950s segregationists, "how limited is the power of law whenever a portion of the community adheres to moral standards which differ from those of the total community."[45] The last decade has vividly illustrated that, even in the absence of revolt, large numbers of disaffected believers bring to politics a rigid and strident persecution complex that destabilizes a political system premised on accommodation and compromise.

## NOTES

1. Julian Jaynes, *The Origin of Consciousness in the Breakdown of the Bicameral Mind* (Boston: Houghton Mifflin, 1976).

2. Bertrand Russell, *Religion and Science* (New York: Oxford University Press, 1961), 8.

3. Edward A. Purcell, Jr., *The Crisis of Democratic Theory: Scientific Naturalism and the Problem of Value* (Lexington: University Press of Kentucky, 1973), 75.

4. 708 F.2d 735 (D.C. Cir.), *cert. denied*, 464 U.S. 1056 (1983).

5. Ibid., 740 n.2 (quoting testimony of Abbott Sekaquaptewa).

6. 108 S.Ct. 1319 (1988).

7. Ibid., 1326.

8. Ibid.

9. For accounts of native American challenges to federal land use decisions, see Milner Ball, "Constitution, Courts, Indian Tribes," *American Bar Foundation Research Journal* 1987: 1; Note, "Indian Religious Freedom and Governmental Development of Public Lands," *Yale Law Journal* 94 (1985): 1447 (student author).

10. Frank v. State, 604 P.2d 1068 (Alaska 1969).

11. E.g., People v. Woody, 61 Cal.2d 716, 394 P.2d 813, 40 Cal. Rptr. 69 (1964); Arizona v. Whittingham, 19 Ariz. App. 27, 504 P.2d 950 (1973), *cert. denied*, 417 U.S. 946 (1974).

12. Employment Division v. Smith, 110 S.Ct. 1595 (1990).

13. See Reynolds v. United States, 98 U.S. 145, 166 (1878) (dictum).

14. E.g., Hardin v. State, 188 Tenn. 17, 216 S.W.2d 708 (1949).

15. E.g., Jehovah's Witnesses v. King County Hospital, 278 F. Supp. 488 (W.D. Wash. 1967), aff'd, 390 U.S. 598 (1968); Raleigh Fitkin-Paul Morgan Memorial Hospital v. Anderson, 42 N.J. 421, 201 A.2d 537, cert. denied, 377 U.S. 985 (1964).

16. E.g., Davis v. Beason, 133 U.S. 333 (1890); Reynolds v. United States, 98 U.S. 145 (1878).

17. Braunfeld v. Brown, 366 U.S. 599 (1961).

18. Bob Jones University v. United States, 461 U.S. 574 (1983).

19. United States v. Lee, 455 U.S. 252 (1982).

20. Goldman v. Weinberger, 475 U.S. 503 (1986).

21. Employment Division v. Smith, 110 S.Ct. 1595 (1990).

22. E.g., Hobbie v. Unemployment Appeals Commission of Florida, 480 U.S. 136 (1987); Sherbert v. Verner, 374 U.S. 398 (1963).

23. Trans World Airlines v. Hardison, 432 U.S. 63 (1977). See also Estate of Thornton v. Caldor, 472 U.S. 703 (1985).

24. Wisconsin v. Yoder, 406 U.S. 205 (1972).

25. E.g., Mozert v. Hawkins County Board of Education, 827 F.2d 1058 (6th Cir. 1987), cert. denied sub. nom. Mozert v. Hawkins County Public Schools, 108 S. Ct. 1029 (1988); Smith v. Board of School Commissioners, 827 F.2d 684 (11th Cir. 1987).

26. Cantwell v. Connecticut, 310 U.S. 296 (1940). See also Widmar v. Vincent, 454 U.S. 263 (1981).

27. For development of this theory, see William Marshall, "The Case Against the Constitutionally Compelled Free Exercise Exemption," Case Western Reserve Law Review 40 (1990): 357; William Marshall, "Solving the Free Exercise Dilemma: Free Exercise as Expression," Minnesota Law Review 67 (1983): 545.

28. Mark V. Tushnet, Red, White, and Blue: A Critical Analysis of Constitutional Law (Cambridge: Harvard University Press, 1988), 257–69.

29. Peter Berger, A Rumor of Angels (New York: Anchor, 1970), 6.

30. Milner Ball, Lying Down Together: Law, Metaphor, and Theology (Madison: University of Wisconsin Press, 1985), 182 n.16 (paraphrasing Karl Barth).

31. Stanley Hauerwas, A Community of Character (South Bend, Ind.: Notre Dame University Press, 1981), 45.

32. Michael J. Perry, Politics, Morality, and Law (New York: Oxford University Press, 1988), 180–82. See also Mircea Eliade, The Sacred and the Profane: The Nature of Religion, trans. Willard R. Trask (New York: Harcourt Brace Jovanovich, 1959), 100–13 passim.

33. Perry, Morality, Politics, and Law, 182.

34. Kent Greenawalt, Religious Convictions and Political Choice (New York: Oxford University Press, 1988), 155.

35. Joseph Campbell, The Power of Myth, ed. Betty Sue Flowers (New York: Doubleday, 1988), 40–41.

36. For an overview of cognitive dissonance theory and its antecedents, see Morton Deutsch and Robert M. Krauss, Theories in Social Psychology (New York: Basic, 1965), 62–76.

37. Berger, Rumor of Angels, 6.

38. James Boyd White, When Words Lose Their Meaning: Constitutions and Reconstitutions of Language, Character, and Community (Chicago: University of Chicago Press, 1984), 4.

39. See Richard John Neuhaus, *The Naked Public Square: Religion and Democracy in America*, 2d ed. (Grand Rapids, Mich.: Eerdmans, 1986), chapt. 14.

40. Harold Berman, *The Interaction of Law and Religion* (Nashville, Tenn.: Abingdon, 1974), 95–96.

41. Robert N. Bellah, *The Broken Covenant: American Civil Religion in Time of Trial* (New York: Seabury, 1975), 45–49.

42. H. McClosky and A. Brill, *Dimensions of Tolerance: What Americans Think About Civil Liberties* (New York: Russell Sage Foundation, 1983), 133.

43. Ibid., 133–34.

44. Neuhaus, *Naked Public Square*, 133.

45. Reinhold Niebuhr, *Christian Realism and Political Problems* (New York: Scribner, 1953), 23.

# Chapter 6

# Reconciliation or
# Repression?

In Part I, we described the persistent religious vitality of American private life despite the general absence of significant religious influence in American public life, noting the threats and dilemmas that this paradox poses both for religion and for public life. At the outset of Part II, we discussed the historical development of secular public life in the United States, together with the common and mistaken belief that all of American society is moving towards secularism. If Americans are not becoming more religious, they certainly are not becoming less so. We then moved to establish the strong hold that religion can have as an unconscious phenomenon, and the deep alienation experienced by many religious Americans because of secularism of public life.

If religion is here to stay as a significant phenomenon in American life, and if significant numbers of its most fervent believers are becoming alienated from American public life, then a serious confrontation between religious Americans and the secularism of American public life is inevitable. The custodians of public life can be expected to try to confine religion to the private sphere. This would likely increase the degree of dissatisfaction, alienation, and radicalization of religious Americans that is already present to some degree. How would America react to the existence of a radical religious movement in its midst?

There are several possibilities. One is that radicalized religion might be repressed, brutally and violently if necessary. Repression might well eradicate religious radicals, and could do away with some religions altogether. Unless religion were wiped out completely, however, repression would breed still further radicalization among the believers that remained. Thus, if repression is not wholly successful in controlling radical religion, violent religious revolution becomes more likely. Another, more hopeful possibility is that religion might be accommodated in public life. The custodians of public life might accept the alienated, radicalized believers into public life rather than repress them. Accommodation defuses radical fervor with the message that government and society recognize and respond to the radicals' concerns. Thus, the need to destroy existing institutions and start over loses its urgency.

## PUBLIC SECULARISM AND RADICALIZED RELIGION

What do we mean by a "confrontation"? As we have described, for many years the influential actors and institutions in public life have proceeded as if the secularization hypothesis were true. Public education, electronic and print media, government, politicians, and intellectuals all go about their business with the unspoken but unquestioned assumption that religious belief is the remnant of a bygone superstitious era that, sooner or later, will fade away in the face of a brave new scientific world.

The secularization hypothesis, however, does not capture the ways in which large numbers of religious Americans relate to the world. Their religious beliefs are not fading. While they may feel that their way of life is increasingly inconsistent with the style of American life assumed and preferred by public culture, this is usually thought by them to indict public culture rather than religion. In other words, for many religious Americans, public life depicts an America that has departed from traditional religious ways of life which past generations of Americans honored and obeyed, in favor of the false gods of humanism and science.

At various junctures, then, secular public culture and private religious life are bound to conflict. At best, public culture reacts to public assertions of the relevance of religious belief with condescension. To public culture, religious people are those too insecure to make their own decisions; believers feel safer depending on God and his spokespersons to make their life decisions, rather than relying on their own abilities. Believers are thought to be intellectually ignorant and psychologically dependent. And the reaction of public culture often goes beyond mere disdain. When believers assert themselves in public life, the conventional wisdom of public culture can treat these assertions as invasions; religious people are soldiers in a foreign army whose occupation of the public square threatens the rationalism and empiricism that lie at the base of liberal thought.

The antipathy between secularism and religion runs in both directions. For their part, religious people often are suspicious of public culture. Anti-intellectualism is a common attribute of conservative religions, especially fundamentalist ones. Committed to a system of belief under which God penetrates into every corner of their lives, they have little use for ways of life that ignore or resist this divine influence. Their perception of a moral canyon between the their "Kingdom of God" and the secular "Kingdoms of Babylon" reinforces and sharpens their feelings of alienation. Thus, when public culture acts to bar them from participating in public life, it only confirms their perception that sin and corruption govern the world and persecute the church.

The conflict of which we speak, then, is not one in which each side holds moral and intellectual respect for the other. It is not a fight in which the combatants generally believe that they share common ground or even mutual respect. Consider political disagreements in Congress or state legislatures over public policy issues. The disputants, despite their disagreements, more or less respect each other and the legislative institution to which they all belong. By contrast, the Williamsburg Charter observes that "recent controversies over religion and public life have too often become a form of warfare in which individuals, motives, and reputations have been impugned."[1]

Religion generally is not respected by the custodians of public culture; it is not thought to rest on an equal intellectual foundation with secular approaches to life. On the contrary, as the superstitious vestige of an outmoded lifestyle, religion is at best thought quaint, and at worst ignorant. Quaint or ignorant views, of course, need not be taken seriously. In the same way, religion fails to respect public culture, which is thought to have cut itself off from the one source that could save it. Secularism, in the view of many believers, is the consequence of human arrogance in claiming the knowledge and ability to live free from transcendent influence. This kind of polarized conflict between irreconcilable worldviews creates the potential for a descending cycle of alienation and violence. Religious people feel persecuted by the secularism of public life, which erodes their allegiance to the norms, practices, and institutions which characterize that life.

As religion comes into increasing conflict with the custodians of public life, those custodians perceive it to be a threat to business as usual, and become more vigilant in policing the boundaries of public life against intrusions of religious influence. Such efforts, in turn, enhance the perception of religious people that the dominant public institutions of American public life are committed to eradicating religion, and inevitably deepen their alienation and dissatisfaction with it. "Each side's excesses," states the Williamsburg Charter, "have become the other side's arguments; one side's extremists the other side's recruiters. The danger is that, as the ideological warfare becomes self-perpetuating, more serious issues and broader national interests will be forgotten and the bitterness deepened."[2]

## LIBERAL NEUTRALITY AND RADICALIZED RELIGION

Religious people are doubly frustrated when they participate in public life. First, they face the presumption that they should not be in public at all, at least not as self-consciously and unapologetically *religious* people. Second, what they say is not heard, because the religious viewpoint is rarely taken as something to be considered on its own terms. Only when religion threatens the political establishment with the tools of democracy—i.e., when it marshals votes—does it get listened to. Then, however, it is not heard as religion, but as power.

Take the ARM litigation, to which we briefly referred in Chapter 1. In this lawsuit, the Abortion Rights Mobilization, Inc., or ARM, sought to silence the Roman Catholic bishops in the United States on the issue of abortion by seeking to have their tax-exempt status revoked by the Internal Revenue Service. The effort ultimately failed, but only after years of bitter litigation. That it was undertaken at all is instructive. ARM's theory was that the prolife activism of the bishops constituted partisan political activity which is prohibited to tax-exempt persons and institutions. If ARM had prevailed, the bishops would have been forced to choose between fighting a practice which they believe to be murder, and guarding their financial resources, which would have been severely depleted by a loss of their exemption from federal income taxes.

Note how ARM shows disrespect not only for the bishops' prolife position, but also for their attempt to articulate it publicly, by challenging the appropriateness of the bishops' speech rather than its substantive merits. Their attack on that position was not that the bishops are simply wrong on abortion, although that clearly is ARM's belief. ARM made no arguments explaining the superior morality of the prochoice position, and how that morality supersedes the life of the fetus. Instead, the message sent by ARM through its litigation is that the bishops should be punished merely for deigning to speak publicly on this issue at all. The bishops were not given the respect one accords equal participants in public debate over the morality of abortion, but instead were treated as gatecrashers who had not been invited to the debate in the first place. ARM refused to listen to what the bishops were saying, preferring instead to attack their right to say it.

There is, of course, the argument that ARM does not have a tax exemption in its fight to protect abortion rights, so why should the bishops enjoy an exemption in their fight to cut back such rights? (The short answer, we suppose, is that the bishops are subject to the restrictions of the establishment clause, and ARM is not.) To pose the question at all only underscores how religion has come to be understood, not as a distinctive and valuable moral voice, but as simply another political lobbying group. Can one imagine forcing the northern Protestant abolitionists of the 19th century to choose between their outspoken opposition to slavery and their tax exemption? Even more sobering, can one imagine the altered course of history had any such effort succeeded in muting or silencing that opposition?

It is one thing to make one's best argument and lose. In a democracy, if other people are not persuaded by one's arguments, there is little else to be done. Even on critically important issues, those who feel like they have had a full and fair hearing in the political arena can usually take their losses with some grace and resignation despite the unavoidable disappointment. However, if people believe that they have failed to persuade because the dominant culture prevented their voices from being heard at all, then the grace and resignation that accompany the loss of a fair political fight is replaced by frustration and anger at having been cheated of the chance of victory.

One interpretation of events surrounding the rise of the prolife movement in the 1970s illustrates this point. Under this account, by the late 1960s most of the states were beginning to move toward more liberal abortion laws. At this point, the prolife movement barely existed as a cohesive entity, let alone a politically powerful one. California's liberal abortion law—which permits abortions in most circumstances—was signed into law during this period by none other than Ronald Reagan, then the governor of California. It was not until after his emergence as a political conservative with a national following that Reagan became a born-again prolifer. By then, the contours of the debate on abortion, as well as its participants, had been considerably transformed. In a series of decisions beginning with *Roe v. Wade* in 1973, the Supreme Court had constitutionalized the right to an abortion. Thereafter, access to abortion did not depend on the actions of a democratically elected legislature, but instead upon the constitutional decisions of unelected federal judges appointed for life. Thus, opponents of abortion felt themselves abruptly deprived of the chance to persuade others of the rightness of their antiabortion views through the democratic process.

*Roe v. Wade* and its progeny galvanized the prolife movement into action. The decision became a rallying cry for the formation of prolife political action groups. The weak and unimportant political force represented by the prolife movement prior to 1973 quickly grew into a fervent, dedicated, and powerful lobby. Moreover, the decision united theologically disparate groups such as Catholics, fundamentalist Protestants, Mormons, and orthodox Jews, groups that generally perceive themselves as having little in common and that in other contexts are often hostile to one another. In attempting to settle the question of abortion "once and for all," the Supreme Court may actually have prolonged and polarized the debate by helping to forge the prolife movement. (This is not the first time in American history that a decision of the Court has backfired in this manner; the 1858 *Dred Scott* case, in which the Court presumed to settle the issue of slavery by depriving Congress of jurisdiction to prohibit slavery in the territories, is widely viewed as a major factor in having caused the smoldering conflict between North and South to erupt into the Civil War.)

Our point here is not that *Roe* was rightly or wrongly decided; rather, it is that by cutting off the possibility, however remote, for prolife people to influence abortion legislation through the democratic process, the Court radicalized the movement.

As we have discussed, the secularization of public life has alienated and radicalized the religious right. Feeling that public culture ignores and ridicules their point of view, conservative religion sees little point in playing by the secular rules laid down by that culture. No culture will enjoy the respect of those whose voices it refuses hear. Those voices become separated from the values of that culture. When they confront the culture, they refuse to abide its conventions, because those conventions are considered instruments of oppression and unfairness. Even the salutary aspects of the culture are trampled underfoot. The culture then becomes involved in a deadly tug-of-war with the counter-cultural movement, deadly because each side seeks to obliterate the influence of the other.

As we have suggested, one response to religious incursions into public life is to redouble efforts to stop those incursions. The separation of church and state is an honored tradition in the United States, even if the strictest versions of that separation have always been held by a distinct minority of Americans. It is a commonplace in Western history to characterize religion as a politically divisive and destabilizing force. One view of the Reformation wars, for example, is that they were primarily motivated by the theological differences between Protestants and Catholics. The putative lesson of this history is that the more that religion intrudes into the secular domain of public life, the more forcefully government and politics must respond in attempting to keep public life secular and, therefore, "safe" from the threatening influence of religious belief.

This safety, however, is illusory. Even subtle pressures to keep religion private and out of public business can create—indeed, have created—frustration and animosity among religious people. Lately, religious people have vented their anger by assaulting the traditional rules of a variety of public traditions and institutions which heretofore have been predominantly secular, such as electoral and legislative politics. Some religious activists have even appropriated civil disobedience as a tool for advancing their agenda. The results of this challenge and response have not been satisfactory by any standard. Defenders of secularized public life continue to paint those who make public arguments from religious premises as dark subversives who threaten to destroy "the American way." In their turn, religious activists have grown increasingly insensitive to the fears and objections of those who do not share their beliefs.

The danger is that the cultural pressure exercised by public actors against religion and in favor of secularism might escalate beyond ignorance or harassment to more overt repression. This is not as unlikely as one might think, from either a theoretical or a practical standpoint. Law professor Steven D. Smith has recently suggested that modern government reflects three stages or modes of dealing with dissent, which approximate the evolution of liberal political theory from the medieval era through the Enlightenment.[3] Smith describes the first stage as "preliberal," characterized by an official orthodoxy or ideology coupled with the repression of dissent. This approximates the attitude of the medieval church and kingdoms prior to the Reformation. The next stage is "tolerant," under which the official orthodoxy remains, but dissent is not repressed. This corresponds to 17th century England following passage of the Act of Toleration, which legalized worship outside of the established Church of England but imposed certain civil disabilities on religious dissenters. Similar developments occurred in some European countries at about this same time. The third stage is "neutral" or "equal," under which the official orthodoxy and the repression of nonconformity are both abandoned. Modern American liberalism purports to be this third kind of government.

One might think that a regime in which all pretense to official orthodoxy is abandoned would be congenial to religious belief and practice. In fact, however, this is not the case. In the first place, ideological orthodoxy is not really abandoned under such a regime; instead, an ideology of neutrality or "no ideology" is merely substituted for the particular religious or other ideology that preceded it, much the same as the Enlightenment merely substituted rationalism and science for God as the foundation of modern social life.

Liberal neutrality presupposes that all moral choices are relative to the position of the chooser; there is no "right" or "wrong" about morality, at least as far as the government is concerned. Thus, potent ideological enterprises like churches—which do teach moral rights and wrongs— represent a serious threat to modern government and its ideology of neutrality. When they attempt to participate in public life on the basis of their moral beliefs, they threaten the fundamental assumption of moral relativism that underlies the ideology of neutrality.

Despite the rhetoric of equality and neutrality sounded by American liberals, the United States is not in the third of Smith's stages, but rather in the second. The current orthodoxy of American public life in general and American government in particular is the orthodoxy of moral neutrality. Religious individuals and groups are permitted to dissent from this orthodoxy, but that does not change the confident belief of the custodians of public culture that all right-thinking people subscribe to the relativism that is presupposed by such neutrality. More ominously, the political distance from repression of dissent in defense of the orthodoxy is greatly reduced in the "tolerant" stage from its extent in a genuine "equality" stage.

Violent repression of religious dissenters is not impossible. The world is barely 50 years removed from the release of darkness from the soul of Nazi Germany expressed in its systematic attempt to exterminate European Jewry. More to the point, even in the United States Americans of Japanese descent were summarily driven from their homes and imprisoned in inland detention camps for most of World War II to guard against an imagined invasion by the Japanese navy—this despite the fact that at no time during the war did the Japanese ever have the capability to invade the American mainland. And even if they had posed such a threat, it is doubtful that this would have justified the wholesale and indiscriminate revocation of the constitutional rights of full *citizens* of the United States.

Lesser incidents of violence and harassment (with equally dubious justifications) directed at left-wing, civil rights and antiwar activists by the federal government are documented well into the 1970s. Persecution and exploitation of racial and ethnic minorities, together with physical and cultural violence against women, are constants in the equation of American social life. In light of all this, there can be no assurance that religious groups are immune from the same sort of persecution under the right circumstances.

Perhaps the most significant factor raising the possibility of repression of a radicalized American religion is, ironically, the lessening of East–West tension that has accompanied the liberalization of politics in Eastern Europe and the Soviet Union. The Soviet threat of world domination that the United States has lived with since World War II is extinct. Thus, the expenditure of vast sums of money to deploy troops and to develop nuclear and other weapons systems to counteract this threat should no longer be necessary. Yet it is not clear that there will be any substantial "peace dividend" to spend, because it is not clear that there will be significant cuts in military spending in the United States.

Some have interpreted the dramatic changes in the Eastern bloc countries as having resulted from the macho toughness projected by the United States during the Reagan administration. In this view, two factors caused the Soviets to sue for peace. First, Reagan's unprecedented peacetime expansion of the American defense forces could not be matched by the lumbering and inefficient Soviet economy. Second, during Reagan's administration, the United States overcame the fear of foreign intervention that it had lived with since Vietnam, and appeared increasingly willing to intervene militarily in other countries, either directly with its own forces or indirectly through surrogates. For the first time in a generation, the United States was prepared to defend its national interests abroad militarily as well as diplomatically.

This "peace through strength" interpretation of recent international events severely undercuts attempts to reduce defense spending; on the contrary, it suggests that continued success in the international arena depends upon maintaining a credible threat of foreign intervention against the enemies of the United States, even if the principal enemy is no longer the Soviet Union. At the same time, the bloated military–industrial complex in the United States has been thrown into crisis with the transformation of the Soviet threat. A reduction in the development and manufacture of weapons systems would mean a reduction in profits. If the Soviet Union can no longer serve as a justification for the expenditure of hundreds of billions of dollars on defense, then a new justification is needed lest the beneficiaries of this spending go broke.

Thus it has developed that as the American taste for large-scale international confrontation has declined, its taste for more focused and intense regional intervention has increased. The 1980s saw full-scale (and widely popular) invasions of Grenada and Panama, as well as support of the Contra insurgents against the Sandanistas in Nicaragua and the Aquino government against a military coup in the Philippines. National defense now encompasses "surgical" antiterrorist strikes like the bombing of Libya and the midair kidnapping of Palestinian terrorist Abu Nidal. Among the most recent deployments of the military is that against drug traffickers. Arms and material are being supplied to various South American countries, and rumors persist of the possibility of direct American intervention against drug lords living abroad.

In the face of the crisis of American drug use, proposals to use the military to police our national borders and to fight drug activities in domestic urban areas are now openly advocated. These proposals are troubling because the same weapons and tactics that succeed in narrow and carefully controlled operations against indigenous regional enemies of the United States will also prove effective against those whom it considers to be its domestic enemies. Thus, as the military retools to adapt to the changed international environment, it will simultaneously adapt itself to domestic police actions. Once the military is deployed against one domestic target, like drug smugglers and pushers, it can be deployed against any such target.

This, in fact, is one of the arguments made by opponents of domestic military deployment, even to combat as serious a problem as illicit drugs. The too-recent experiences of Japanese American internment and violence and surveillance directed at civil rights and antiwar protestors and black activists during the 1960s and 1970s suggest that all one needs is a plausible argument that the target threatens domestic peace and tranquility. Indeed, commentators and even judges speak candidly of the "drug exception" to the Constitution, referring to the pattern of legislative and judicial decisions in drug cases which severely undercuts many of the individual liberty protections contained in the Bill of Rights. The perception of crisis can provide a justification for eliminating even constitutional rights.

The possibility of domestic violence against religious groups is one of the more disturbing implications of the city of Philadelphia's police action

against MOVE several years ago. MOVE was a religio-political movement composed almost exclusively of African Americans who practiced
a vague naturalistic theology focused on re-creating premodern social
and cultural practices in a modern urban setting. MOVE members ate
special diets of uncooked fruits and vegetables, lived in polygamous,
communal family units, did not bathe or otherwise observe modern health
conventions, and did not allow their children to attend school. They also
possessed weapons and displayed occasional violence. Their congrega-
tion in a number of apartments in an African-American residential area
of Philadelphia became a source of controversy, leading to accusations
by residents that the loud, vulgar, and bizarre lifestyle of MOVE members
had ruined the neighborhood. Finally, on the pretext of saving the
children in the MOVE community, the Philadelphia police attempted
forcibly to enter the apartments of MOVE members by dropping a bomb
from a helicopter on one of the apartment entrances and rushing the
apartment under cover of the explosion. (The operation was coordinated
by a city official who had served two tours of duty as a career Army
officer in Vietnam.) The fire caused by the explosion destroyed over 50
homes, and 15 MOVE members burned to death, including four children.[4]

Continued exclusion of religion from public life could easily bring
such anger and frustration to the boiling point. As religion becomes ever
more alienated from public life, its internal restraints on the use of
violence also become less constraining. Religion is only one of many
human endeavors with a long and honored tradition of martyrdom, and
the temptation to "make a statement" with some spectacular antisecular
violence could eventually prove too much to withstand. As religion grows
increasingly radical, it could by its own actions grow into the justification
for antireligious domestic military action.

Thus, a scenario for violent domestic conflict between secularism and
religion could easily be constructed: A state increasingly equipped and
adept at combatting urban violence, set against one or more religious
communities pushed beyond their breaking points by exclusion from
public life. Americans are already predisposed to believe the worst about
religiously motivated terrorists in the international arena. Should such
groups ever direct their attention away from their bases in Northern
Ireland and the Middle East to targets in the United States, this stereotype
would be strongly reinforced; one could hardly rely on American law
enforcement to draw fine distinctions between these international religious radicals and the homegrown variety.

## THE HYPOCRISY OF SECULARISM AND NEUTRALITY

One threat of a secular public culture, then, is that enforcement of its secularism by rigorously confining religion to private life might radicalize religion to the point of violence, triggering the secular state to respond in kind. There is, however, another, more subtle danger that inheres in such a culture: it sows the seeds of its own ideological destruction.

How we talk about ourselves eventually changes us. "Words are not idle," argued social critic Norman O. Brown. "They have consequences."5 How we act as individuals, communities, and a nation depends to a large extent on our individual and collective self-concepts. If, for example, we continually conceive of ourselves as aggressive and warlike, and talk about ourselves in terms of this individual and collective self-concept, we should not be surprised to find ourselves growing more aggressive and attracted to war. This may hold true even for those whose original sensibilities might even have been passive and nonviolent; they will find themselves under constant moral pressure by the dominant conceptions of self and nation.

If religion remains excluded from public life and culture—from politics, law, government, media, and school—Americans will slowly lose the ability to make the linguistic and conceptual distinctions called for by religious language. Consider, for example, the distinction "pagan" versus "nonpagan." That distinction is meaningless in contemporary American society. To be sure, we still know what the words mean—a pagan is someone who worships idols, and thus a nonpagan is someone who does not.

But the social and cultural setting for this meaning and the distinction is gone. What idols? What did it mean to believe in them? How were these beliefs integrated into everyday life? What did it mean to dissent from such beliefs? Were there consequences? Did dissenters have alternative beliefs? What were they? The answers to these and other related questions are known only by those who specialize in ancient societies, and even these scholars cannot know for certain how those societies were organized and functioned. For the great bulk of moderns, the distinction is without meaning. The pagan concept of surviving by means of spiritual deities whose presence and power extend to every part of life is simply incomprehensible to most of modern humanity.

So it would be with religion. When we no longer permit any public description of ourselves—individually, communally, or nationally—as religious, it will not be long before we become linguistically incapable of describing ourselves in such terms. The dissonance experienced by religious believers as the result of the secularism of American public life may cause them to abandon their religion rather than their government. Religious people may succumb to the pressure of secularism, forsaking their beliefs or emasculating them to the point that they have little relevance and force in contemporary life. This would remove any serious threat to contemporary American society from religious violence at the cost of eliminating religion as a significant social force not only in public life, but also in private.

To those committed to a secular public culture in the United States, this seemingly would be no great loss. We will argue in Chapter 9 that such a view of the demise of religion is shortsighted even for avowed secularists. For now, we wish to emphasize a different point. That Americans collectively may choose to abandon religion is a potential consequence of life in a pluralistic society. Various ideas and lifestyles compete in the "marketplace of ideas," and those that do not effectively meet the needs of the people so as to be continually chosen by some portion of them will eventually die out. American cultural history is littered with failed experiments in living which did not survive their founding generation. It is possible to conceive of a good life that is without religion, and a choice by Americans to abandon religion, while perhaps lamentable, is a possible byproduct of freedom.

Under the scenario we have sketched, however, a choice against religion would not be clearly free, in the sense of being the authentic and uncoerced decision of an autonomous individual or community. Indeed, for a large portion of the American people, freedom has been and continues to be exercised rather consistently in favor of the religious life, at least in their private lives. The pressure and perceptions of secularism being imposed on private American life by public life and culture, however, might eventually "wear down" this religious commitment, so that the choice to abandon religion would not be an authentic reflection of the personality and aspirations of the chooser.

Certainly Americans will have difficulty remaining religious if American culture does not preserve a language of belief. "Myths are so intimately bound to the culture, time, and place," writes Joseph Campbell, "that unless the symbols, the metaphors, are kept alive by constant recreation through the arts, the life just slips away from them."[6] Thus, by failing to preserve the memory of what it means to be religious, a secular public culture could result in the extinction of religion. The secularization hypothesis might then come true, but not as a result of enlightened choice so much as the result of cultural oppression. As feminist Paula Gunn Allen has observed, "the root of oppression is loss of memory."[7]

This possibility has serious implications for the liberal conceptions of both state and individual. At the center of liberal political theory is the goal of creating a state that maximizes individual choice. Thus, one of the strongest liberal policies underlying the protection of speech, self-expression, and lifestyles from state interference is the fear that governmental suppression or distortion of information and ideas through censorship will lead to "wrong"—that is, ill-informed, irrational, or inauthentic—judgments by individuals. If one excludes religious speech and expression from public life, this very liberal fear is realized—people end up making decisions that are less informed, often less rational, and certainly a less authentic expression of their individuality than those that they would have made in the presence of unrestrained religious conceptions of reality.

Whether religious or not, each person must eventually decide for herself what part she will allow God to play in her life. Such a profound judgment cannot be made in the absence of the religion alternative. A second option of public culture to latest American religious revival, then, is to reconcile with it. Public culture can accommodate religious believers rather than repressing them. By this we mean that public life and culture invite, or at least accept, religion and religious belief in public life as legitimate and appropriate participants therein. This response is more likely and certainly more desirable, we believe, for two reasons. First, accommodation and acceptance are wise—they soften the radical edge that religious believers otherwise are in danger of sharpening in response to cultural repression and violence. Second, accommodation is truer to the humanistic roots of American liberalism than is repression. Accommodation is what enables all Americans, if they wish, to choose the dream.

## NOTES

1. *The Williamsburg Charter* (Williamsburg, Va.: n.p., 1988), 14. The Charter was drafted by a diverse group of religious and nonreligious people who are committed to working out a legitimate role for religion in American public life.

2. Ibid.

3. Steven D. Smith, "The Restoration of Tolerance," *California Law Review* 78 (1990): 305, 308–12.

4. For accounts of this incident, see Ted Guest, "Nightmare in Philadelphia," *U.S. News & World Report* (May 27, 1985): 20; Philip Weiss, "Goode, Bad and Ugly: How He Bombed in Philadelphia," *The New Republic* (June 10, 1985): 12.

5. Quoted in *Voices and Visions*, ed. Sam Keen (New York: Harper & Row, 1974), 36.

6. Joseph Campbell, *The Power of Myth*, ed. Betty Sue Flowers (New York: Doubleday, 1988), 58.

7. Paula Gunn Allen, *The Sacred Hoop: Recovering the Feminine in American Indian Traditions* (Boston: Beacon, 1986), 213.

Part III

# The Reconciliation of Religion to American Public Life

# Chapter 7

# **Choosing the Dream**

Until the early 20th century, religion was a significant public influence in the United States. In contemporary America, however, public life has become largely secular even though religion remains vital and significant in American private life. It has been a long time since religious groups uncontroversially participated in public life. Yet if the discourse of American public life is to remain truly open so as to afford Americans with the fullest range of moral choices, public discourse must be founded upon religious knowledge as well as upon the secular knowledge that is already abundantly present in public life. How can this be done? Even if Americans were to decide that the secularism of public life is undesirable, it is not clear how it can be changed. At the least, we need to develop new habits of public citizenship. If religion is properly to become a legitimate participant in American public life, one must determine how religion is to participate—that is, how we are to conceive of religion and understand its claims as a public phenomenon, as opposed to a private one.

Religious belief can be "real" in a way that is both understandable and meaningful even to nonbelievers, if one focuses less on the claimed source of religious experience and more on the effects of that experience in the lives of believers and on the society in which the believers live. Religion should remain what it claims to be—communication from God—but evaluation of its further claims to truth and knowledge should be evaluated according to their usefulness in living a full and satisfying human life.

## THE SPIRITUAL STERILITY OF MODERNISM

Not so long ago, religion was an important, even the dominant, means of obtaining knowledge about the world. Medieval humanity was not limited to reason and empiricism in discovering how the world works; it also obtained knowledge by crediting an external source linked to the transcendent reality of religious beliefs. It is familiar history that the medieval church too zealously guarded its claim to authority in imparting knowledge, and in defense of that claim suppressed many truths. Despite this, religious experience—the reception of knowledge from God—has been a powerful positive force in Western history. Virtually every aspect of contemporary Western culture is to some extent traceable to the Jewish and Christian religious traditions.

This influence of religion on Western history and culture did not wholly disappear in the 20th century. The Progressive movement, fueled in part by fundamentalist Protestant churches, was the dominant political movement of the early part of the century. Nevertheless, as the 20th century wore on, the participation of religious individuals and groups in public life grew increasingly controversial. As we described in Chapter 3, the United States eventually reached the point where secularism became the dominant mode of discourse in public life, with religious arguments largely confined to private life.

Accordingly, in the United States it is now presumed that few people seek religious experiences in the strong sense of the phrase (or, at least, that no right-thinking person ought to). Indeed, the presumption is that experiences claimed to be religious are really something else—the consequences of phenomena largely if not fully explainable in terms of a secular discipline like history, psychology, or politics. Nevertheless, many people in the United States *do* seek after religious experience; indeed, the spiritual sterility of modern life has left many Americans desperate for it. Because they cannot find religion in public life and culture, they turn to substitutes.

In an interview in the late 1960s, Norman Brown explained the attraction of hallucinogenic drugs as their ability to access extraordinary experiences beyond the objective measure of rationality and empiricism: "I don't use drugs," stated Brown. "However, it is obvious that we need a breakthrough to a visionary reality, a poetic vision."[1] In an interview at about the same time, Joseph Campbell acknowledged that "drugs have uncovered the unconscious depths in a society that is lopsidedly rational and evaluative."[2] More recently, Campbell has blamed the denial of transcendence in modern society for having turned people to drugs as the only way to access religious experience.[3] Even if the reality of religious experience is denied, people still seek it.

Drugs should not be the only means of accessing spirituality. While in some non-Western traditions drugs are properly associated with spirituality—the peyote rituals of the Native American Church and the opium smoking of some Eastern mystics are two examples—in general drugs only enhance the Western religious experience, they do not create it. As both Brown and Campbell suggest, religious experience is all around; it is only the emphatic denial of its reality that forces one to substitutes in order to access its visionary potential.

One must acknowledge that even secularists accept "visions" of the moral life, so long as they are merely figurative—that is, so long as they are only abstractions with the spiritual origins and dimensions excised. "I have a dream," declared Martin Luther King in his famous speech on racial reconciliation, not "I have *had* a dream." Far more difficult for the secularist to deal with are visions in the strong sense of the word, as revelations from God. As we set out in the Introduction, that is what we intend by the "religious experience"—that experience by which one receives knowledge from God. Admitting that such knowledge is valid seems to require that one accept the reality of its source—the existence of God. To do so, however, would contradict the dominant interpretation of intellectual history in the West, by which the last 500 years are seen as having culminated in the freedom of humanity from the superstitions and violence of religion.

The progress of Western civilization is conventionally measured in large part according to the successful displacement of religion by rationalism and empiricism as the privileged discourses in public life. To publicly recognize the religious experience is to give back the intellectual acreage won by the Enlightenment, the Reformation, and the Renaissance. Hence the vigorous resistance offered by public culture whenever religion seeks reentry into public life: It fears relapse into the medieval mode of religious repression in defense of orthodoxy.

We do not wish to reenact the Middle Ages by undoing the Renaissance, the Reformation, and the Enlightenment, thereby displacing secularism with religion. Rather, we conceive of the readmission of religion to public life without its replacing secularism. Is it possible to accept that the religious experience generates knowledge that is as powerful and as valid as that generated by rationalism and empiricism without regressing to the medieval paradigm of social life in which religious knowledge is privileged over all other ways of knowing? Is it possible to permit the recipients of religious knowledge to articulate their messages publicly without diluting, disguising, or removing their spiritual content? Can American public culture credit religion as what it purports to be—divine communication—and on that basis grant it respect, interest, and (not least) accountability? The implications of these questions are profound. Accepting religion as a full and equal participant in American public life means that the religious experience must be accepted on its own terms, as spiritual and transcendent experience, rather than on the terms of a rationalism or an empiricism which cannot capture and communicate its essential character.

The issue that concerns us here is whether the largely forgotten religious orientations to life and knowledge that once animated Western history and culture can be revitalized into a contemporary account of American life that is public as well as religious. Such an account would frame religious belief as a viable means of dealing with the problems of contemporary life. Religion could then set itself against the hostility exercised by American public culture toward the public claims of contemporary American religion, bearing witness to the moral deficiencies of public culture and suggesting ways in which they could be remedied.

Without such an account, the die is already cast. If religion continues to claim against the protests of secularists that it legitimately can participate in public life *as religion*, history suggests that it will be persecuted and suppressed. Without a national commitment that recognizes the value of religion and the religious experience, there will be nothing to mitigate persecution. Religious people will then either abandon their beliefs and assimilate, or radicalize them and rebel. Faint suggestions of each scenario are evident in the mainline Protestant churches, many of which advocate a political agenda coinciding with that of left-wing Democrats, and the alienated religious right, which militantly fights against conventional social practices and laws. Neither scenario is attractive, but can either one be avoided?

## THE REALITY OF RELIGIOUS BELIEF

To create a contemporary account of religion that allows it space in the public square, one must first choose to recognize the way in which visions of religious transcendence are real. One of the unique characteristics of human personality is a refined and sophisticated capacity to envision better worlds; ideal conceptions of life that do not exist in the temporal, physical world. That such idealizations do not occupy time and space does not, however, make them less real than physical objects that do. In terms of their effect on the lives of their adherents, these ideals and conceptualizations are at least as real as physical objects which exist in time and space; these ideals and conceptualizations constitute the means by which adherents interpret and judge events in temporal life. Law professor Gerald Frug has written that

> people perceive the world by selecting out those things which seem important to them and [then] tailor[ing] their actions to those selected perceptions. . . . The combined process of accommodation of ideas to experience and assimilation of experience to ideas means that, to some extent, the world is made to conform to our ideas and, to some extent, our ideas are made to conform to the world.[4]

In a similar vein, philosopher Hilary Putnam has written that "the mind and the world jointly make up the mind and the world."[5] In other words, the meaning of the observations and experiences that a person accumulates while living in the temporal world depends upon her beliefs, which are themselves shaped and influenced by observations and experiences. Thus, the beliefs that underlie a person's conception of how the world works dictate to a large extent how she sees the world, and how she acts in it. The world, in turn, dictates to a large extent the content of her beliefs.

For example, a social Darwinist and a fundamentalist Progressive at the turn of the 19th century in the United States could both look at the poverty and squalor of the industrial workforce of that era and see very different things. The Darwinist saw the oppression and squalor as inevitable, if not desirable. To her, society no less than biology was about the survival of the fittest. No imperative for moral action came from the Darwinist interpretation of the world of the exploited worker; on the contrary, from the Darwinist perspective the moral imperative was for *in*action, because the Darwinist believed that the world, for all its oppression, was as it ought to be.

The fundamentalist, on the other hand, saw the same thing very differently. Poverty and squalor, in her view, resulted from the abandonment of God and his teachings; they were evidence that American society had broken the divine covenant. The normative solution from the fundamentalist perspective was to return to God by renewing the covenant, ministering to those who were oppressed, and calling society to judgment in accordance with the scriptures. Thus, the very same empirical facts created two very different realities, because each interpreter projected onto those facts very different meanings.

As we have described, for religious people it is their religious beliefs which create the reality against which the events of temporal and physical existence are interpreted. Religion creates a *transcendent* reality—a deeper reality that goes beyond the appearance of temporal physical existence. In Western religion, God stands both outside of human existence and in judgment of it. The idea that the choices and actions one exercises in journeying through life are judged by God, so as to have implications and consequences before birth or after death, meets a compelling human need to know that one's existence is not arbitrary or accidental, but is instead linked to an enduring (and, therefore, more "real") truth and reality. Paul Tillich thus writes that religion "gives us the experience of the Holy, of something which is untouchable, awe-inspiring, an ultimate meaning, the sense of ultimate courage. . . ."[6]

Consider, for example, the Old Order Amish who live in various rural areas of the United States. The Amish believe that God requires them to forsake all aspects of the sinful contemporary world, including the use of most modern appliances. They maintain an 18th century agrarian lifestyle in a 20th century technological world, making a living through farming and related trades while using no electricity, automobiles, telephones, power tools, or other modern machinery and appliances. They also forsake contemporary fashion, dressing instead in unadorned, old-fashioned clothing.

The Amish are motivated by their abiding belief in a God who will punish them harshly if they do not persist in their anachronistic lifestyle, and who will richly reward them if they do. The physical and psychological hardships caused by the incongruence of Amish life with contemporary lifestyles are, therefore, of little moment in light of the eternal consequences of obeying (or disobeying) God's word. The day of judgement is inevitable and cannot be escaped. Conversely, the spiritual peace and satisfaction of conforming one's life to the divine is precious. To the Amish, then, the concepts of "heaven" and "hell" are real, more real than anything in the temporal physical world.

"Reality" is the conception of the world to which people choose to bind themselves in living their lives. It need not be scientifically verifiable, and, in case of belief in a religious reality, may seem fanciful and even bizarre to nonbelievers. However, to those who hold to a religious conception of reality with conviction, the consistency of that belief with the apparent reality of physical existence in time and space is a secondary consideration. Ultimately, it is belief, and not temporality, that signals what is real about the world. Philosopher José Ortega y Gassett argued that a belief must be distinguished from an accepted idea, a scientific truth, for instance. Ideas are open to discussion; they convince by virtue of reason; whereas a belief can neither be challenged nor, strictly speaking, defended. While we hold a belief, it constitutes the very reality in which we live and move and have our being. . . . [Reality is] that which must be reckoned with, whether we like it or not.[7]

The important social question here is not whether God "really" exists, but whether those who live and function in American society believe that he exists. Where there are significant numbers of believers, as there are in the United States, society must take account of the actual and potential impact that these believers and their beliefs have on public life.

At its best, religion promises humanity not only a better life hereafter, but a better way of life here and now. The promise of an existence hereafter that is somehow linked to the here and now is a compelling one, drawing one to consider the eternal implications of choices and actions in temporal physical existence. Often, as with the Amish, this is because theology conditions acceptance into a heaven and avoidance of a hell upon a life lived in conformity to particular religious values. Even in the absence of such rewards and threats, however, belief in a transcendent religious reality often will influence the believer to alter her behavior. Even the mere knowledge of what is right and what is wrong that is conveyed by religious belief can move the believer to choose the right—to "choose the dream" of the better life that is implicit in her religious beliefs.

## RELIGIOUS EXPERIENCE

Thus far, we have considered religion in the light of various secular lamps—from the standpoint of history in Chapter 3, psychology in Chapter 4, rationalism and empiricism in Chapter 5, and social conflict in Chapter 6. Although we have made clear our bias in favor of a public role for religion, we have yet to consider the religious experience on its own terms.

Let us now consider religion by the light of its own lamp, as men and women talking with God, and God talking back. God gives a message to a person, and that person receives the message. The religious person conceives of and relates to the message just as it was received, as a spiritual, transcendent experience rather than as a phenomenon of history, psychology, epistemology, politics, or any other secular discipline. The divine source of the religious experience is what gives it its authority, what makes it worthy of attention and obedience. Religious knowledge is not validated by virtue of its grounding in any intellectual tradition, but rather by virtue of its source in God.

And therein lies a paradox. For the individual who has had a religious experience, the source of the message in God is as important as the substantive content of the message. The knowledge of how one ought to live is compelling because the experience of receiving this knowledge testifies to its origin in God, and not because the moral life revealed by the experience is itself inherently attractive. Indeed, the history of religion is testimony to the opposite—the religious life, as all moral life, is rarely the way of least resistance. "Values do not drive a man," wrote psychologist and Holocaust survivor Viktor Frankl,

> they do not *push* him, but rather *pull* him. . . . Man is never driven to moral behavior; in each instance he decided to behave morally. Man does not do so in order to satisfy a moral drive and to have a good conscience; he does so for the sake of a cause to which he commits himself, or for a person whom he loves, or for the sake of his God.[8]

The strong compelling sense of divine origin in religious experience, however, cannot be objectively or otherwise decisively demonstrated to other people. The mere fact that one person has had a religious experience does not in itself draw another to obey the message received in the experience of the first. Only after the other has undergone her own religious experience does the message become as real and compelling to her as it is to the first. What this means is that the description of an experience as "religious" by a person provides a relevant basis for others to evaluate the fact of the experience as well as its content only when such others also seek and obtain the same experience.

Thus, whether a religious experience is "true" in the sense that its claim of divine origin is real cannot be evaluated in any direct or objective way. There is nevertheless a way in which the truth of a religious experience can be evaluated. The point of religious experience is communication from God about how to live. Since such a communication is of divine origin, the resulting moral knowledge is typically character-ized as "good" or even "best." (God, presumably, does not reveal bad ways to live.) Michael Perry has described moral knowledge as "knowl-edge about how to live so as to flourish, to achieve well-being. More precisely, it is knowledge about how *particular* human beings . . . must live if they are to live the most deeply satisfying lives of which they are capable."9

It is possible for individuals to evaluate whether a religious value system is likely to lead to the "flourishing" or "well-being" of those who practice it. More to the point for a discussion about the role of religion in public life, people can discuss among themselves whether such systems lead to the kind of people and lives that are desirable, or not. Even though the "truthfulness" of a religious experience cannot be evaluated directly on an intersubjective basis, it can be evaluated in terms of the individual and communal life that grows out of that experience. Thus, participants in public life need not inquire of religious experience whether it is "true" or "real" in the specific terms of its claim of divine origin. They need only evaluate the quality of human life that is generated by religious communities centered on religious experience. Thus, the question is not, "Is this 'true'? Did it 'really' come from God?" but instead, "Can we believe this? Does it help where we need help? Does it explain what we need to know? What we want to know? Does it help to live the kind of life we would like to live?" The following sections offer some examples of what we mean by this in the context of specific religious experiences.

### Moses

We start virtually at the dawn of recorded history in the West, with the Hebrew prophet Moses. The full account of Moses's life found in the Old Testament is probably not historical, having been written by later Hebrew scribes and prophets seeking to augment and solidify Moses's reputation as one who communicated with God. Nevertheless, biblical scholars are generally agreed that Moses is an historical figure connected to the core of the Old Testament narrative of the early Hebrews. According to this narrative, the Hebrews—identified in the Old Testament as the descendants of Abraham, Isaac, and Jacob or Israel—were enslaved in the northeastern part of the Nile River delta during the 13th century B.C.E.

There they came in contact with an Egyptian prince of Hebrew descent who discovered his relation to the slaves, intervened on their behalf, and consequently was forced to flee Egypt as a fugitive. The book of Exodus records that this one-time prince, Moses, returned to lead the slaves to freedom, because God spoke to him out of a burning bush and commanded him to do so: "Come now; I will send you to Pharoah and you shall bring my people Israel out of Egypt."10

Moses did return to Egypt, the Hebrews fled their bondage to the promised land, and Judaism, the first great religious tradition of the West, was preserved. Because the Jews have maintained their religious and cultural identity throughout the centuries despite persistent persecution, their history is inextricably intertwined with that of the rest of the world.

## Paul

Perhaps the central figure of early Christianity, after Jesus himself, was the apostle Paul. Although there are no sources on his life outside the letters attributed to him in the New Testament, many of these are believed by scholars to be genuine. Born a Jew, he nevertheless possessed Roman citizenship and was fluent in Greek. As a young man, he enthusiastically united himself with the Pharisees, a Jewish sect which promoted strict adherence to the traditional Law of Moses. To the Pharisees, Jesus and his followers represented a blasphemous challenge to the traditions of the prophets, and Paul zealously worked with other Pharisees to stamp out the Christian heresy.

Christian tradition has it that Jesus appeared to Paul while he was traveling to Damascus to apprehend some Christian converts there, and directed Paul to stop his persecutions.[11] Following this vision of God, Paul abruptly sided with the Christian heretics. In the letter to the Galatians, one of those believed by scholars to have been authored by Paul, he wrote:

> You have heard what my manner of life was when I was still a practising Jew: how savagely I persecuted the church of God, and tried to destroy it; and how in the practice of our national religion I was outstripping many of my Jewish contemporaries in my boundless devotion to the traditions of my ancestors. But then in his good pleasure God, who had set me apart from birth and called me through his grace, chose to reveal his Son to me and through me, in order that I might proclaim him among the Gentiles.[12]

As this passage suggests, Paul became the central figure in preaching the Christian gospel to the "gentiles" or non-Jews.[13] It is, of course, largely because non-Jews eventually accepted Christianity in large numbers that it grew into a major world religion rather than simply fading from the scene like most of the numerous Jewish sects common at the time of Jesus. Moreover, Paul's letters in the New Testament were major theological influences on Reformation figures like Martin Luther and John Calvin.

## Muhammad

The third of the great Western religions, Islam, was founded in the 7th century C.E. by the prophet Muhammad. Born and raised in an impoverished family in Mecca, he was nevertheless a member of one of the leading clans in Meccan society. When he married into riches, he became a major figure in Meccan business and politics. About 610, he had a vision of the angel Gabriel, who declared him to be "the messenger of Allah." Throughout his life, Muhammad received revelations from Allah which were eventually collected and recorded in the Koran. Muslims thus believe the Koran to contain the words of Allah himself.[14]

The influence of Islam in history hardly needs explanation. Conflict between Christianity and Islam in Eastern and Southern Europe, Asia Minor, and the Middle East is a recurring theme of Western history. Although for some time Islam has been one of the world's largest and fastest growing religions—it influenced even the American civil rights movement in the 1960s—its international power and influence did not fully penetrate American consciousness until 1979, when the Ayatollah Khomeini overthrew the Shah of Iran and reestablished an Islamic theocracy in Iran. Islam figures prominently in the contemporary conundrum of Middle East politics.

## John Wesley

John Wesley, the founder of the Methodist Church, was originally ordained to the ministry in the Church of England. Following appointment to one of the colleges at Oxford, he joined and soon led a group of pious students devoted to serious Bible study, frequent attendance at Communion services, and regular performance of good deeds. This earned them the mildly derisive nickname, "Methodists," because of the methodical way in which they went about studying and living the word of God. In 1735, Wesley and his brother traveled to the American colony of Georgia to minister to the colonists and convert the native Americans there. By their own account, they failed because they held only intellectual convictions about the Church, and lacked genuine Christian faith. Returning to England in 1738, Wesley embarked upon a more spiritual examination of the scriptures.

While attending a meeting of the Moravian Church of the Brethren devoted to Luther's commentary on Paul's Letter to the Romans, he experienced a personal witness that he had been saved by the atonement of Jesus: "While [the speaker] was describing the change which God works in the heart through faith in Christ, I felt my heart strangely warmed," Wesley wrote in his journal. "I felt I did trust in Christ, Christ alone for salvation: And an assurance was given me, that he had taken away *my* sins, even *mine*, and saved *me* from the law of sin and death."15 Shortly thereafter, he began preaching to the unchurched masses of the English poor. Methodism gained rapidly among all those who felt neglected by the aristocratic and hierarchical Anglicans. Four years after Wesley's death in 1791, the Methodists broke completely with the Church of England.16

Methodism grew to become one of the major Protestant denominations in both the United States and Great Britain. In addition, Wesley's experience of being reborn free of sin through the atoning sacrifice of Jesus typified for Protestants the spiritual conversion to Christianity. The personal conversion experience has since became the hallmark of evangelical Protestantism. As we have noted, nearly one-half of all Americans can identify such a spiritual conversion in their own lives. Through all of the periodic religious revivals that have gripped America from the early 18th century to the present, the personal witness of having been born again through Jesus has remained a constant.

### Joseph Smith

Joseph Smith, the founding prophet of Mormonism, lived during the Second Great Awakening in an area of upstate New York known as the "burned-over district" because of the frequency and fervor of the evangelical revivals that took place there. As a pious but theologically troubled fourteen-year-old, he describes how he sought divine guidance through prayer about which church he should join. He received a vision in which God himself instructed Smith to join none of the churches, but instead to restore the true gospel of Jesus Christ that had been lost through the ages. Some years later, he published the Book of Mormon, which he described as a scriptural account of God's dealings with the ancient inhabitants of the Americas translated by divine gift from gold plates delivered to him by an angelic messenger. Smith grew into a powerful and charismatic spiritual leader who held together a large religious community through severe persecutions in Ohio, Missouri, and Illinois. He died in 1844, assassinated by a lynch mob.17

The Mormons were a significant force in the settlement of the American West. Following their expulsion from Illinois, they traveled to the Salt Lake Valley in Utah and eventually established other settlements in Arizona, California, Idaho, Nevada, and Wyoming. Mormonism's contemporary significance stems from distinctive beliefs relating to modern revelation and the atonement of Jesus which place Jesus at the center of Mormon worship while at the same time deeply reinterpreting and revising the traditional Christian narratives. With these beliefs, Mormonism has grown into a significant challenge to orthodox evangelical Protestantism in the United States. It is the largest religion founded in the United States, and is among the fastest growing denominations in the Western Hemisphere.

## A PRAGMATIC APPROACH TO RELIGIOUS EXPERIENCE

Despite the otherworldly character of the lives we have just sketched, large portions of their religious experiences remain subject to examination and evaluation. One can, for example, evaluate the consistency of their spiritual testimonies. All of them relate one or more encounters with a God that changed their lives and told them how to live. Many of them endured severe hardships and even death in defense of the truth of their experiences. One can also evaluate the efficacy of the knowledge which they claimed from their experiences. It proved effective in freeing slaves, converting unbelievers, creating devoted communities of followers, subduing wilderness, and writing scripture. These events are there in history, open to study. Perhaps the most important evaluative point, however, is that the knowledge and communities based on these religious experiences have endured. Through the ages, ways of life based upon knowledge gleaned from religious experience have survived and even prospered. However improbable their origins may sound to the modern ear, these ways of life nevertheless work.

In the face of this alone, one might at least admit the possibility that religious experience is real. In any event, the quality of the life of those who have built communities upon the moral knowledge obtained from particular religious experiences is open to examination and discussion. It *is* possible even for nonbelievers to discuss what it means to live as a Jew, a Christian, a Muslim, or a Mormon, and to reach conclusions about whether those who live in accordance with the beliefs and narratives of these religions are flourishing and well—that is, whether they are living the most deeply satisfying lives of which they are capable.

There will be disagreement, to be sure, about the well-being generated by various religious communities, but it is nonetheless a disagreement that is subject to discussion. One need not pass definitive judgment on the truth claims of divine origin; one need only admit that divine origin is possible.

As one might expect, there have been numerous attempts to explain the phenomenon of religious experience by denying or refuting its claim of divine origin. They all examine the life of the person claiming religious experience through the prism of some nonreligious discipline such as psychology, history, sociology, or the like. Rationalizing the revelatory experiences of prophets and saints as the result of epilepsy, for example, is so commonplace that it constitutes a cliché. These secular approaches, of course, undercut the spiritual claims of the one who has had religious experience. To the extent that her revelations, and her followers' fidelity to them, can be explained in terms of some secular discipline, doubt is cast upon the claim of the prophet that God actually talked to her.

Moreover, secular approaches distract from the more important question whether communities built upon the experience recommend a viable and valuable way of life. Whether one who claims religious experience has actually received revelations from God is a question whose truth is not subject to any authoritative, objective discourse. Having said that, however, it hardly follows that their claims of divine communication are necessarily false. The inability authoritatively to determine the source of one's claimed revelations need not prevent discussion and evaluation of the substantive merits of life based upon the experience. The question of religious experience is then transformed, from whether it is genuinely of divine origin, to whether the actions, theology, and community which it spawns are coherent and desirable. In other words, if someone were to make claims of religious experience in public life, the issue should not be whether the claims are "true," but rather whether they "work." Certainly in the United States millions upon millions of religious people can point to their communities of belief as beacons of strength and hope set in the darkness of a corrupting and alienating world. In this sense, religious experience is a legitimate source of knowledge about how to live. Some people will choose to follow the knowledge afforded by a particular religious life; many others will choose not to be religious at all. At least, however, one should be able to choose.

If public culture can accept religion and the religious experience as full and equal participants as we have described, America can enter a new age. It can proceed to develop public criteria for judging the merits of religion in a transformed and integrated world, a world in which all experiences are recognized, accepted, and judged as desirable or not, irrespective of their origin and epistemology. No longer need we conceive of the world as religion set against secularism, fact against value, subject against object, public against private. All of these are instead circumscribed into a single whole. Normative criteria for judging the varieties of human experience will still exist—criteria of rationality for the intellectual world, of science for the scientific world, of art for the artistic world, of *religion* for the *religious* world. But none of these should be privileged, presumed "better" than the others at describing how one ought to live. Instead, they should simply coexist in one ecumenical world, displaying the full richness and potential of human diversity as they are variously combined and transformed in individuals and communities.

## NOTES

1. Quoted in *Voices and Visions*, ed. Sam Keen (New York: Harper & Row, 1974), 35.

2. Quoted in ibid., 74.

3. Joseph Campbell, *The Power of Myth*, ed. Betty Sue Flowers (New York: Doubleday, 1988), 61.

4. Gerald Frug, "The City as a Legal Concept," *Harvard Law Review* 93 (1980): 1059, 1079.

5. Hilary Putnam, *Reason, Truth and History* (Cambridge: Cambridge University Press, 1981), xi.

6. Paul Tillich, *Theology of Culture*, ed. Robert C. Kimball (New York: Oxford University Press, 1978), 9.

7. José Ortega y Gassett, "Concord and Liberty" in *Concord and Liberty*, trans. Helene Weyl (New York: Norton, 1963), 9, 18–19.

8. Viktor Frankl, *Man's Search for Meaning: An Introduction to Logotherapy*, trans. Ilse Lasch (Boston: Beacon, 1959), 174.

9. Michael J. Perry, *Morality, Politics and Law: A Bicentennial Essay* (New York: Oxford University Press, 1988), 11.

10. Exod. 3.11 (New English Bible).

11. Acts 9 (New English Bible).

12. Gal. 1.13–16 (New English Bible). See also 1 Cor. 15.8 (New English Bible).

13. For an introduction to Paul's life and thought, see T. R. Glover, *Paul of Tarsus* (New York: Doran, n.d.).

14. For an introductory biography of Muhammad, see W. Montgomery Watt, *Muhammad: Prophet and Statesman* (Oxford: Oxford University Press, 1961).

15. *The Journal of John Wesley: A Selection*, ed. Elisabeth Jay (Oxford: Oxford University Press, 1987), 34–35 (from entry describing events of May 24, 1738).

16. For an overview of biographical approaches to Wesley's life, see Richard P. Heitzenrater, *The Elusive Mr. Wesley*, 2 vols. (Nashville, Tenn.: Abingdon, 1984).

17. The most widely used biography of Joseph Smith is Fawn McKay Brodie's psychohistorical work, *No Man Knows My History: The Life of Joseph Smith, the*

*Mormon Prophet* (New York: Knopf, 1946). For biographies more sympathetic to Smith's claim of divine inspiration, see Richard L. Bushman, *Joseph Smith and the Beginnings of Mormonism* (Urbana: University of Illinois Press, 1984); Donna Hill, *Joseph Smith, the First Mormon* (Midvale, Ut.: Signature, 1977).

*Chapter 8*

# Beyond Rationalism

Throughout most of the 20th century, the American intellectual tradition has labeled religion irrational and subjective. This is one of the legacies of the Enlightenment, which replaced religion with science as the foundation of knowledge. Modern intellectuals habitually devalue ways of knowing that cannot be verified by experiment and observation. It is true that the truth claims of religion cannot be put to experimental tests like theories of physics or biology. One cannot empirically prove that God talks to people, because one can't ever seem to produce God in the act of talking. It is also true that many religious truth claims cannot be rationally proven in any meaningful way, although reason often informs religious belief, and the relation between reason and religion is closer than many suppose.

At the same time science, for all its claims to empiricism and rationality, also must admit that knowledge cannot be reduced to observation and logic. The objectivity of science has proven illusory. Twentieth-century physics has decisively demonstrated that the very act of measurement affects the behavior of the object or phenomenon being measured. Odd as it may seem, observing the world makes it into a different place than it would have been if one had not attempted the observation. Indeed, observation may actually give existence to the observed object in the first place—that is, the object being observed literally has no existence until observation is attempted.

Even scientific objectivity is a point of view, and thus not so distant from the intuition and spirituality that characterize religious belief.

Moreover, the subjectivity and irrationality of religion are much exaggerated. While one cannot hope to produce God in the act of talking, the consequences of obeying his words are open to observation and analysis, as we argued in Chapter 7. Does religion work? Does it direct us to a way of life that is viable in the contemporary world? Does it lead to results that one can judge socially or otherwise desirable? Does it make us better people? These are all questions that can be addressed by the rational and objective conventions of contemporary intellectual thought.

## THE CONVENTIONAL VIEW OF RATIONALITY AND OBJECTIVITY

What does it mean to talk of "rational" ways of thinking? Concepts of rationality are difficult and highly complex. It is not our task to formulate an original version of rationality. Rather, we wish only to describe rationality to the extent that is necessary to capture its use and importance to contemporary culture, in particular contemporary public culture.

During the Middle Ages, religion was among the most rational of intellectual activities. Thomas Aquinas and the Scholastics attempted to systematize all of medieval theology. While their proofs of religion were internally consistent—that is, the conclusions they drew followed from the premises they asserted—the assumptions on which those proofs were based had no necessary connection to the observable world. Thus, the knowledge they purported to provide was of little practical use. For example, one can prove that the sun revolves around the earth if one assumes, among other things, that earth and its inhabitants are at the center of God's attention. This bit of logical knowledge is limited in its usefulness, however, if the earth is not in fact at the cosmic center. After all, conclusions that follow from their premises are useful in learning about the world only if the premises themselves relate to what one can observe about the world.

Unfortunately, the empirical validity of logical premises was not a general concern of medieval theology; it cared more for logical consistency. This ignorance of empiricism was at the heart of the controversy between Galileo and the medieval church. Galileo claimed to have disproved by observation, rather than by deduction, the geocentric theory which held that the sun revolved around the earth. Geocentricity was a fundamental premise of the logical structure of medieval theology, which saw no need for empirical investigation. Thus, Galileo's empirical observations were rejected because they undermined medieval theology.

This sort of "detached rationalism" was severely criticized in the early 20th century, when the intellectual ascendance of science reached its apex. Such criticism followed from the fact that logical premises did not necessarily reflect what one could observe about the world. Deductive logic came to be perceived as trivial. Logic alone permitted one to declare meaningless absurdities to be true: " 'All gostaks are doshes,' and 'All doshes are galloons.' Then, quite properly and flawlessly, the logician could deduce that 'All gostaks are galloons.' Although the statement was logically unassailable . . . , it proved nothing."[1]

All systems of rational or deductive reasoning came to be viewed as useless except to the extent that one could show that they described what existed in the physical world. "*A priori* rationality . . . did not mean 'that which agrees with experience, but that which we find ourselves inclined to believe.' "[2] This strong orientation to empiricism led 20th century scholars to reject as a basis of useful knowledge all arguments from premises that could not be observed. "Only propositions that were experimentally, observationally verified were in any sense true."[3]

So it is that in contemporary society the term "rational" does not simply mean "logically consistent." To be rational in today's world, one must make arguments that resonate with the experiences of most other people. Kent Greenawalt writes that a concept or process is thought to be rational if it "rest[s] on reasoned arguments whose force is generally understood. [I]t is clear that an argument that a particular society treats as rational at least reflects very widely shared canons of reason within the society. At a minimum, if most people in a society regard a judgment as irrational, it offends accepted ideas of reason."[4]

As a general proposition, then, "rational" might mean "consistent with a widely shared understanding about what is reasonable." A concept or process would be rational if it could be explained in a way that is convincing and persuasive to most people. An explanation will be convincing and persuasive in this sense if it refers to events or phenomena that most people have experienced. A concept or process would be irrational if it could be explained only in a way that is unconvincing or unpersuasive to most people.

Suppose that Jane is about to leave home with an umbrella. If in response to the question, "Why are you taking an umbrella?" Jane answers "Because it looks like it is going to rain today," the questioner will be satisfied (assuming that it *does* in fact look like rain). Even if the sun is shining brightly, the answer "Because the weather report predicts rain later today" will satisfy the questioner, since weather reports are usually correct, even though not perfect. (And even if they are not usually correct, people commonly rely on them anyway.) The questioner's own personal experiences with what the world looks like when it is about to rain, or with the reliability of reported weather predictions, enable her both to understand and to be persuaded by Jane's explanations for her behavior. If Jane's explanations match what the questioner's experiences have taught her about how the world works, Jane's answers will make sense to the questioner.

Contrast these two possible answers to the query why Jane is taking an umbrella with a third: "Because I expect the sun to shine all day." At best, this answer is puzzling. Based upon the questioner's likely experience, Jane's explanation suggests the *absence* of any need to bring an umbrella, since there can be no apparent reason to take an umbrella to protect one from the rain if one does not expect rain. From this standpoint, then, Jane's statement is irrational. "Rational knowledge," writes physicist Fritjof Capra, "is derived from the experience we have with objects and events in our everyday environment. It belongs to the realm of the intellect, whose function it is to discriminate, divide, compare, measure, and categorize."[5] If an explanation is not consistent with how most people have experienced the world, it will not be taken as rational—that is, it will not be understood or believed.

There is a close relationship between rationality and objectivity. A concept or process is said to be "objective" if it accurately describes the world "without ever mentioning the human observer."[6] Contrast the statement "The car is red," with the statement "Jane thinks the car is red." The first is an objective statement, because it purports to describe the car—the object of the observation—without taking account of the possibility of imperfections or biases in the observer's abilities. It thus implies fact and certainty. The second statement, however, is subjective, because it describes only what the observer—the subject who is observing—believes she sees, and does not purport to describe what color the car "really" is. Jane, after all, may be colorblind, or hallucinating, or inattentive.

Subjectivity thus implies opinion and ambiguity. In objective thinking, the uncertainties of observation and perception are divorced from the reality one is describing; the attributes of the object of inquiry are assumed to exist independently and apart from the attributes of the observer. In subjective thinking, observation and perception are integrated with the described reality; the attributes of the object of inquiry depend, at least in part, on the attributes of the observer.

Because the question whether concepts or processes are rational of necessity depends on how most people interact with the world, rationality is typically thought to be an objective judgment. Thus, if in response to the umbrella query, Jane answers (without elaboration) that she is carrying an umbrella because she expects a sunny day, her conduct will be judged irrational. This explanation simply does not coincide with most people's experiences with the weather. The possibility that, based on Jane's own experiences, carrying an umbrella on a sunny day makes sense to her is not likely to save her from the judgment of irrationality if her experiences are idiosyncratic and peculiar.

Because the judgment of rationality depends on how most people experience the world, those experiences are usually taken as how the world *is*—that is, the experiences of most people are taken to constitute objective knowledge, rather than subjective opinion, about "reality." Objectivity thus leads to what is known as the "correspondence theory of truth." Under this theory, "the-way-things-really-are" is assumed to exist independent and apart from any observer. Something is "out there," and however and whatever it is, it is assumed to "be" independent of how (or even whether) it is accurately perceived by any human agent.

Law professor Roberto Unger has written that "what distinguishes men from one another is not that they understand the world differently, but that they desire different things even when they share the same understanding of the world. There is only one world of facts and only one form of understanding, fundamentally alike in everyone. A man may know more or less about the world, but whenever two men know something truly what they know is the same thing."[7] The thrust of the initial Enlightenment criticism of medieval scholasticism was that its proofs were trivial or irrelevant except to the extent that they corresponded to what "actually existed."[8] In this view, the "truth" of thoughts, beliefs, concepts, or other mental images "consists in their correspondence with reality."[9]

Similarly, philosopher Mortimer Adler defines truth as "a relationship of agreement or correspondence . . . between what a person thinks, believes, opines, or says to himself and what actually exists or does not exist in reality. . . ."[10] (Hereafter, when using "truth" and "reality" in the manner intended by the correspondence theory—that is, as singular, independent, and unique—we will spell them with capital letters, as "Truth" and "Reality.")

Few philosophers these days accept the validity of the correspondence theory as a test of truth or rationality.[11] This does not mean, however, that it is without influence in the contemporary world. Michael Perry describes the correspondence theory as the one most likely held and believed by the "man-in-the-street,"[12] and literary theorist Hazard

Adams has observed that the correspondence theory is "pervasive in public science and the public eye."[13] Correspondence theory remains the dominant test of truth and rationality among the general population, if not among philosophers. Statements, beliefs, and explanations that are inconsistent with the description of Reality conceived and understood by most people are deemed by most people to be false.

## FLAWS IN THE CONVENTIONAL VIEW

Although the foregoing account of rationality and objectivity may be the most widely believed, it is flawed. One of the strongest challenges to the account comes from a one-time ally, science. It is common to conceive of science as representing one pole of a continuum between rationality and objectivity, on the one hand, and irrationality and subjectivity, on the other. (Religion is a common candidate for representing the other pole.) As it turns out, however, placing science at the rationality/objectivity end of the continuum is problematic. Upon examination, science turns out not to be objective, and rationality without objectivity turns out to be something considerably different than the conception of rationality presupposed by the correspondence theory.

In the face of the Enlightenment challenge to medieval epistemology, the church attempted to maintain control over the discovery and dissemination of knowledge about the world by shrouding it in mystery and incomprehensibility. To the extent that the world could be explained at all, only the specially trained and dedicated Catholic clergy could discern the "true" explanations. By Enlightenment standards, medieval ways of knowing tended to be both irrational and subjective. By contrast, Enlightenment scientists sought to explain the world in terms of everyday experience ("experi-ments") whose validity could be tested by reenactment and duplication. Among contemporary scientists, an important test of the validity of a scientific concept remains whether the supporting experimentation can be repeated by others with the same result. Enlightenment epistemology, in contrast to its medieval counterpart, aspired to both rationality and objectivity.

The explosion of industrial and technological progress in the 19th and 20th centuries was closely related to new discoveries about the nature of the world that were exposed by the rationalism and empiricism that germinated in the Enlightenment. It is not surprising, then, that the last 100 years has seen the rise of a virtual "cult of science." Science came to be seen as the ultimate answer to every problem. Until recently, the strongest and most definitive adjective one could use to indicate truth or reality was "scientific," as in, "It's a *scientific* fact."

Assertion that something had been proved scientifically came to be understood as a claim that the related knowledge is rational and objective—and for that reason virtually indisputable. Although in recent years the belief that science can eliminate all of the ills of modern society has been tempered, belief in the rationality and objectivity of science persists, at least in the popular mind. Science is not thought to be biased or subjective, a matter of opinion, but rather neutral and objective, describing how the world *is* regardless of how one perceives it. In contemporary American society, science constitutes one of the most privileged discourses about the nature of the world.

Ironically, at the same time that science captured popular imagination in the 20th century, other developments in science scarred its veneer of rational and objective inquiry into the "true" nature of the world. In theoretical physics, for example, Einstein's theory of relativity holds that there is no absolute frame of reference for measuring time: "Time is, in fact, elastic and can be stretched and shrunk by motion. Each observer carries around his own personal scale of time, and it does not generally agree with anybody else's."[14]

Accordingly, the speed at which a body moves in space and time is relative to the position of the observer making the measurement. (Hence the name of the theory, "relativity.") Time can no longer be regarded as absolute, fixed, or universal; it "can stretch and shrink, warp and even stop altogether. . . . Clock rates are not absolute, but relative to the state of motion or gravitational situation of the observer."[15] Thus, two events that appear simultaneous to one observer might not appear simultaneous to another observer.

More recent advances in quantum physics have yielded comparable results. One famous quantum principle is known as the Heisenberg uncertainty principle after Werner Heisenberg, the physicist who discovered and elaborated it. This principle states that the *location* of an atom or subatomic particle and its *momentum*—that is, its mass times its velocity—cannot both be calculated at the same time. For example, one cannot simultaneously measure where an electron is and how it is moving. This limitation appears not to be a function of imprecise measurement, but a fundamental limitation related to the nature of the world. If one measures location, the electron exhibits the characteristics of a *particle*, which is how most people conceive of subatomic structures. If one measures momentum, however, the electron exhibits the characteristics, not of a particle, but of a *wave*, like radio or electromagnetic waves which we generally do not conceptualize as being composed of particles:

> The fuzzy and nebulous world of the atom only sharpens into concrete reality when an observation is made. In the absence of an observation, the atom is a ghost. It only materializes when you look for it. And you can decide what to look for. Look for its location and you get an atom at a place. Look for its motion and you get an atom at a speed. But you can't have both. The reality that the observation sharpens into focus cannot be separated from the observer and his choice of measurement strategy.[16]

In other words, the determination of what to measure—location or momentum—alters the characteristics of the atom—particle or wave. Indeed, one might say that the atom does not exist at all—has *no* characteristics—until measurement is attempted!

A related phenomenon is the Einstein-Podolsky-Rosen effect, which describes the behavior of light particles or "photons" under certain circumstances. The decay of an atom or a subatomic particle can produce two photons that travel away from each other in opposite directions and that contain opposite spins. Such a pair of photons is said to be "polarized." Inexplicably, any attempt to measure the directional spin of one polarized photon is instantaneously and inexplicably communicated to its counterpart, the photon moving in the opposite direction, so that the counterpart photon exhibits the opposite spin.

The act of measurement alters not only the behavior of the photon being measured, but also the behavior of its counterpart. As one science writer has described it, "the traditional quantum theory interpretation of this paradoxical result is that the polarization of the photons, like the position of an electron, simply does not exist in any sense until it is measured. This implies that there is no such thing as an objective reality—the act of observation is an essential part of the phenomenon being observed."[17]

All of these phenomena have been widely verified by scientific experiment and are firmly grounded in theory. If they are true, then even the most careful scientist cannot be objective; even scientific knowledge depends to some extent on the biases of the observer, and, therefore, is to that extent subjective. Moreover, to the extent that these phenomena cannot be explained, they lack the commonsense indicia of rationality. The idea that reason and experiment can uncover and demonstrate objective truths on which the universe rests is thus an illusion, even (or perhaps especially) in science.

The implications of relativity and quantum theory are profound. Together, the two theories prove that it is impossible to observe the universe without also participating in and altering it. "The commonsense view of the world, in terms of objects that really exist 'out there' independently of our observations, totally collapses in the face of the quantum factor."[18] Different people experience the world in different ways. (Indeed, they experience different worlds!) Thus, there is no way to approach Reality that is not colored and distorted by the observer: "It is the impossible attempt to step outside our skins—the traditions, linguistic and other, within which we do our thinking and self-criticism— and compare ourselves with something absolute."[19] The correspondence theory of truth fails because, as Michael Perry has succinctly stated, "we lack access to Reality."[20]

## A CRITIQUE OF THE CONVENTIONAL VIEW

From this insight has come the post-modern critique of the correspondence theory. In contrast to the correspondence theory, postmodernism denies the possibility of neutrally demonstrating Reality. To the postmodernist, reason and science can be as suspect as religion. Hazard Adams writes that

the idea of empiricism as the foundation of science has been largely dismissed. The whole realm of the philosophy of science has become a battleground since the notion has been put forward that science and its processes are governed to some considerable extent by the social and institutional fabric in which the work is carried on and the nature of the work is constituted. [T]he role of the scientist has been hemmed in and structured according to laws that have little to do with the old idea of the autonomous subject investigating an object.[21]

Thus, Mark Edmundson suggests that "one might think of postmodernism as trying to get done what its practitioners had sensed modernism had failed to do; that is, to purge the world of superstition in every form."[22] In postmodern thought, the Enlightenment project is a failure, having only succeeded in replacing worship of God with worship of science. The assumption of contemporary American public life is that secularist discourse naturally, neutrally and inevitably reveals

Reality. Postmodernism, on the other hand, asserts that there is no privileged discourse that can lay bare Reality and affirm the Truth; *all* forms of human discourse are biased and skewed by ideological allegiance.

In the postmodern view, "certain meanings are elevated by social ideologies to a privileged position, or made the centres around which other meanings are forced to turn."[23] An "ideology," in turn, is the "largely concealed structure of values which informs and which underlies our factual statements. . . ."[24] In other words, what constitutes knowledge, and therefore what is considered Real, is not a function of nature—"the-way-the-world-really-is." Rather, what counts as knowledge is a function of culture, politics, and power—"the-way-the-world-is-seen-by-those-who-control-it." Those in a position to influence culture and politics impose their view of Reality on the less powerful by dressing their view up in the guise of nature. But this view is not natural so much as it is merely comfortable: "The familiar world of facts is simply the world of a very familiar version. It is the world of a theory so old, so entrenched, so successful, that it is for us the world that is "there," that needs explaining (but not warranting). . . ."[25]

Postmodernism does not necessarily entail denial that Reality exists, only denial that one can know in any objectively decisive way what Reality is like. Nor does it necessarily deny that the usefulness of human knowledge may derive from some relation or correlation of theory or belief to Reality. What postmodernism protests is the privileging of certain kinds of knowledge as "real," and other kinds of knowledge as "unreal," based on some claimed access to Reality. Any such claim must be false because one simply cannot demonstrate to another the nature and content of Reality.

The mere fact that a person has experienced the world in a way that differs from the experiences of most people should not automatically render that person irrational. In a postmodern world, there is no privileged position from which one can glimpse an undistorted view of Reality. Thus, the fact that one conceives of the world in an idiosyncratic way does not make her irrational. Rationality, rather than being an objective measure of consistency with widely shared experience and understanding, must be transformed into a subjective measure of consistency with the individual's own experiences and understanding.

So long as one can supply an explanation which renders her behavior consistent with her own experience and understanding, she is rational. To continue with our earlier example, even if it is clear that rain is not expected or even possible, Jane might nevertheless provide a reasonable explanation of her behavior by suggesting an alternative use for the umbrella—"I'm going for a walk later today, and want to use the umbrella for a walking stick" or "I expect the sun to be hot, and want to use the umbrella for a sunshade." These are both plausible uses for an umbrella, even if they happen to lie outside the experience of the questioner. Although the questioner may never have used an umbrella in this way, and may never have even thought of using the umbrella in this way, Jane certainly has, and the coherence of the explanation with her prior thoughts or actions renders her explanation rational. In fact, the experience of the questioner is largely irrelevant. Even if Jane supplies a highly idiosyncratic explanation—"This was my mother's umbrella, and I like to carry it on walks to feel close to her memory"—it can still be rational so long as Jane has told the truth. In other words, if the umbrella really *was* her mother's, and really *does* evoke in Jane memories of her mother, it makes perfect sense for Jane to carry the umbrella when she wants to remember her mother.

This account of rationality is called the "coherentist" or "holist" conception: "Whether it makes sense for a particular person to believe something—whether the belief is "rational"—depends on what else she believes."[26] The coherentist conception takes into account the whole web of experiences and beliefs held by the actor, and pronounces her rational to the extent that her actions are consistent with those experiences and beliefs.

If the correspondence theory of truth cannot work, what can take its place? How does one evaluate truth claims in a postmodern world? As we suggested in Chapter 7 in the specific case of religion, pragmatism is one strategy. Philosopher Richard Rorty writes that for the pragmatist, "knowledge is power, a tool for coping with reality. . . . He drops the notion of truth as correspondence with reality altogether, and says that modern science does not enable us to cope because it corresponds, it just plain enables us to cope."[27]

The value of a particular way of conceiving of the world can be judged on whether or not it "works"—whether or not it helps its adherents live better lives. "Better," of course, requires some standard of evaluation. A conception of how the world works can be viewed as useful or valuable to its adherents, if it fits with what those adherents think they already know about the world at the same time that it illuminates and transforms that prior understanding.[28] This is a judgment that, in most cases, can only be made subjectively—that is, by individuals based upon their personal experiences with and understandings of the world.

Under a coherentist conception of rationality, by which evaluations are made pragmatically and subjectively, religious experience has a considerable element of rationality, more than it is commonly given credit for. As we discussed in Chapter 7, though one cannot directly observe or test the core of religious experience—God talking to humanity—one can certainly see and measure the consequences of a religious experience in the lives of its adherents: what the experience caused them to do, how it has ordered or reordered the various aspects of their lives. Religious people live in temporal society, even though their most important personal referents may be transcendent. Thus, the fruits of religious experience—how it causes people to live their lives—are open to rational inquiry and subjective choice by individuals making such inquiries.

In this light, the distinction between science and rationality, on the one hand, and religion and irrationality, on the other, becomes blurred. Professor Greenawalt, for example, has argued that it is rational to credit the validity of a source of knowledge when the source consistently yields good results. This is true even when one cannot rationally demonstrate how and why the source generates the results. Thus, a police chief rationally can rely on a psychic to solve crimes if in the chief's experience the psychic's responses to questions about a criminal investigation are usually right. That is, the reliance on the psychic is explainable by a reason that can be understood in terms of widely held or demonstrable experience—the psychic has been right in the past. The fact that the chief cannot explain *how* the psychic gets the right answers does not render reliance on the psychic irrational, so long as the chief calls on the psychic solely because of his past track record.[29] (On the other hand, if the chief calls on the psychic because the chief believes in the occult, and not because the psychic is usually right, then Greenawalt would conclude that the chief is acting irrationally, pursuant to a reason that cannot be demonstrated—that there is the power in the occult.) By this reasoning, people who believe in the power of prayer solely because, in their experience, prayers are usually answered, are not acting irrationally.

More generally, those who adhere to a particular religious lifestyle because it enables them to flourish, to live well, in the alienation and corruption of the modern world also are acting rationally. In both cases, so long as the action is congruent with the believers' prior beliefs and experiences, it makes sense to believe that the religious action is effective in living a "better" life—that the action *works*.

This style of inquiry and analysis is not unlike that used in much scientific research, such as experimental work in quantum physics. Many subatomic particles cannot be seen or observed directly; the reality of their existence is thought to be demonstrated when experiments involving the particles yield results predicted by theoretical models constructed on the assumption that the particles do, in fact, exist. Perhaps, then, public culture should not be so quick to assume that religious belief is wholly beyond the realm of reason. Whether religion delivers on its promise of a better way of living here and now, and not just hereafter, is open to rational examination and inquiry, even if the belief in God is not. It is always open to the critic (and the cynic) to examine the fruits of the religious experience.

Postmodernism is the key to understanding the dominance of secularism in public life, and the confinement of religion to private life. The triumph of Enlightenment thinking in 20th century America meant that secular discourse became the privileged way of talking in public life. Secularism (and in particular science) came to be viewed as the exclusive way to uncover Reality and demonstrate Truth. Religious ways of discovering knowledge about the world became discredited and, as a result, were no longer taken seriously in public contexts—hence their banishment to private life.

If the postmodern insight is correct, then secularism has no exclusive claim as the language of American public life. The exposure of science and secularism generally as enterprises with a subjective dimension, together with an understanding of the rational dimension of religious belief and experience, refutes even secular arguments for keeping religious discourse out of public life. If there is to be authentic political dialogue, then both religious and secular voices properly assert themselves in public life.

## THE LIMITS OF RATIONALITY AND OBJECTIVITY

It remains true that the core of religion—the religious experience itself—remains hidden from view. However much we may analyze the consequences of that experience in the lives of its believers, the experience itself can be understood only by those who personally undergo it. Translating the religious experience into a common language so that it may be made the subject of rational discourse is a poor substitute for the experience itself. As Joseph Campbell observed, "the best things can't be told because they transcend thought."[30] Similarly, Fritjof Capra writes that "the Eastern mystics repeatedly insist on the fact that the ultimate reality can never be the object of reasoning or of demonstrable knowledge. It can never be adequately described by words, because it lies

beyond the realms of the senses and of the intellect from which our words
and concepts are derived."[31]

The difficulty becomes even more acute when we realize that we even
think in language. Thus, even one's own concept of herself is skewed by
the language that she speaks:

> I still need to use [language] when I look into my mind or search my
> soul, and this means that I will never experience any "full communion"
> with myself. It is not that I can have a pure, unblemished meaning,
> intention or experience which then gets distorted and refracted by the
> flawed medium of language: because language is the very air I breathe,
> I can never have a pure unblemished meaning or experience at all.[32]

There is a profound point here. The meaning of human life—or of any
human's life—not only cannot be reduced to logic and empiricism, it may
not even be reducible to language. Ironically, scientists understand this
as well as anyone. Even as they attempt to reduce matter to its most basic
particles, and the forces of nature to a single unified explanation, they
remain in awe of the inexpressible beauty of the universe as a whole.

"There is a growing appreciation among scientists," writes physicist Paul
Davies, that "however important it may be to understand the fundamental
simplicity at the heart of all natural phenomena, it cannot be the whole
story."[33] Science historian Thomas Kuhn has persuasively argued that
progress in science is not achieved incrementally by the accumulation of
technological data. Instead, science leaps forward upon the backs of creative
and imaginative metaphors that originate more often in intuition than in
experiment or data.[34] One physicist has suggested that because physics
depends so much on insight and intuition, it is really a form of art.[35] And
in a statement that faintly hints of the discredited methods of the medieval
scholastics, another scientist has contended that "it is more important to have
beauty in one's equations than to have them fit experiment. . . ."[36]

Rationality is an inherently reductionist enterprise, seeking to translate
the experiences of life into language and then to break them down into
their fundamental logical components of premises and arguments. While
it is clear enough that understanding and knowledge about the world can
be gained from rationalist systems, it should also be clear that understanding and knowledge may lie elsewhere as well. "Not everything in
reality," wrote Paul Tillich, "can be grasped by the language which is
most adequate for the mathematical sciences."[37]

Similarly, Richard Neuhaus writes that "most of the things that we
believe really matter—love, community, honor, purpose in life—are not

subject to scientific measure and control."[38] James Boyd White argues that those aspects of life which are subject to the epistemology of rationalism occupy a relatively unimportant place in the lives of most humans: "The region that can be ruled by the methods of logic and science, and by the parts of the mind that function in these ways, is, after all, rather small. . . . For good or ill, much the larger part of human life must proceed without the certainties these two forms of reasoning provide."[39]

Communication of knowledge gained from religious experience, in particular, cannot depend solely on rational exposition if its full richness is to be conveyed. To the extent that it is dependent on language, it must employ less direct means of communication, such as poetry or narrative. Indeed, the quality of religious experience might be better conveyed without direct reliance on language at all, as through music, art, ritual and feeling. The modern world (as contrasted with the postmodern one), with its continued reliance on the illusion of objectivity and the correspondence theory of truth, considers religious knowledge unreliable. Yet if objectivity and rationality do not circumscribe human experience, then the subjectivity and inexplicability of religious experience are hardly flaws, let alone fatal ones. Understandings of faith and love, for example, would be impoverished were we restricted in expressing them to scientific language, or any language at all. It is precisely because religion is neither objective nor wholly rational that it is able to "open up levels of reality that otherwise are hidden and cannot be grasped in any other way."[40]

For example, one cannot fully understand Jesus's life and the normative power of the doctrines he preached if one focuses solely on the historical "facts" of his existence. It is the scientifically inexplicable and linguistically unrepresentable *belief* that Jesus was God made flesh who overcame sin and death that draws Christians to strive to live according to his words. The irrational and the subjective elements embodied in religious belief and experience enable people to see and to understand concepts that can only be inadequately expressed, if at all, by the rationality and objectivity that inhere in a common language. The irrationality and subjectivity of religion, far from being weaknesses in the contemporary world, are instead its strengths.

"Objectivity" about human reality is an illusion. There is no privileged position in the universe from which any human being can definitively pronounce the true nature of things. Indeed, the pretense to such a position obscures the truth as often as it reveals it. The truth of knowledge comes to be judged on the extent to which it corresponds to the privileged pronouncements. Propositions are deemed erroneous, not because of their intrinsic lack of merit, but rather because they do not conform to unquestioned and unquestionable assumptions about "external reality" that have been articulated by the privileged mouthpiece. Such an approach creates a dogma that values conformity over truth, and thereby discourages creativity and inhibits imagination.

In one of history's ironies, the Enlightenment, which was supposed to rescue the world from the dogmatic conformity of medieval religious oppression, instead created its own dogma of rationality and objectivity. Religious conceptions of reality are implicitly devalued by secular public culture to the extent that they cannot be rationalized and objectified. As an explanation for what is happening in the world, religious experience is rarely taken seriously. Yet when a religious experience is claimed to have caused dramatic social changes and effects, one possible explanation must be that the experience was real. As we argued in Chapter 7, if the United States is to reach beyond the sterile secularism of modern American public life to a postmodern society in which no discourse is privileged, it must begin to admit the possibility that religious experience truly occurs, not as the pathetic hallucinations of the unbalanced or insecure, but as what it claims to be—God talking to humanity. The subjectivity and irrationality that characterize the religious experience can hardly count against the knowledge which this experience brings to individuals and to society.

## NOTES

1. Edward A. Purcell, Jr., *The Crisis of Democratic Theory: Scientific Naturalism and the Problem of Value* (Lexington: University Press of Kentucky, 1973), 89.

2. Ibid., 47 (quoting Charles Sanders Pierce).

3. Ibid., 48.

4. Kent Greenawalt, *Religious Convictions and Political Choice* (New York: Oxford University Press, 1988), 57.

5. Fritjof Capra, *The Tao of Physics: An Exploration of the Parallels Between Modern Physics and Eastern Meditation*, 2d rev. and updated ed. (Boston: New Science, 1985), 28.

6. Ibid., 57.

7. Roberto Mangabeira Unger, *Knowledge and Politics* (New York: Free, 1975), 40.

8. Cf. Purcell, *Democratic Theory*, 53.

9. Garth L. Hallett, *Language and Truth* (New Haven: Yale University Press, 1988), 14.

10. Mortimer J. Adler, *Six Great Ideas* (New York: Macmillan, 1981), 43.

11. E.g., Terry Eagleton, *Literary Theory: An Introduction* (Minneapolis: University of Minnesota Press, 1983), 143, 146; Hallett, *Language and Truth*, ch. 2; Perry, *Morality, Politics and Law*, 40–42; Stewart Candlish, "The Truth About F.H. Bradley," *Mind* 98 (1989): 331, 339.

12. Perry, *Morality, Politics, and Law*, 40.

13. Hazard Adams, *Antithetical Essays in Literary Criticism and Liberal Education* (Tallahassee: Florida State University Press, 1990), 274.

14. Paul Davies, *God and the New Physics* (New York: Simon & Schuster, 1983), 120.

15. Ibid., 123.

16. Ibid., 103.

17. David H. Bailey, "Scientific Foundations of Mormon Theology," *Dialogue: A Journal of Mormon Thought* 21 (Summer 1988): 61, 63.

18. Davies, *God and the New Physics*, 107.

19. Richard Rorty, *Consequences of Pragmatism: Essays, 1972–80* (Minneapolis: University of Minnesota Press, 1982), xix.

20. Perry, *Morality, Politics, and Law*, 41.

21. Adams, *Antithetical Essays*, 228–29.

22. Mark Edmundson, "Prophet of a New Post-Modernism: The Greater Challenge of Salman Rushdie," *Harper's Magazine* 279 (Dec. 1989): 62, 63 (emphasis added).

23. Eagleton, *Literary Theory*, 131.

24. Ibid., 14.

25. Ruth Anna Putnam, "Creating Facts and Values," *Philosophy* 60 (1985): 187, 194.

26. Michael J. Perry, *Love and Power: The Proper Role of Religion and Morality in American Politics* (New York: Oxford University Press, [forthcoming] 1991).

27. Rorty, *Pragmatism*, xvii.

28. See Catherine Elgin, "The Relativity of Fact and the Objectivity of Value" in *Relativism: Interpretation and Confrontation*, ed. Michael Krausz (Notre Dame, Ind.: Notre Dame University Press, 1989), 86, 91.

29. Greenawalt, *Religious Convictions*, 60–62.

30. Joseph Campbell, *The Power of Myth*, ed. Betty Sue Flowers (New York: Doubleday, 1988), 49.

31. Capra, *Tao of Physics*, 29.

32. Eagleton, *Literary Theory*, 130.

33. Davies, *God and the New Physics*, 225, 229.

34. See Thomas Kuhn, *The Structure of Scientific Revolutions*, 2d ed. (Berkeley: University of California Press, 1970).

35. Davies, *God and the New Physics*, 221 (quoting David Bohm).

36. Ibid., 220–21 (quoting Paul Dirac).

37. Paul Tillich, *Theology of Culture*, ed. Robert C. Kimball (New York: Oxford University Press, 1978), 54.

38. Richard John Neuhaus, *The Naked Public Square: Religion and Democracy in America*, 2d ed. (Grand Rapids, Mich.: Eerdmans, 1986), 135–36.

39. James Boyd White, *When Words Lose Their Meaning: Constitutions and Reconstitutions of Language, Character, and Community* (Chicago: University of Chicago Press, 1984), 22.

40. Tillich, *Theology of Culture*, 56.

# Chapter 9

# Beyond Historicism

As we discussed in Chapter 5, American public culture points to what it believes to be the irrational and subjective nature of religion to justify its exclusion from public life in general, and from the political process in particular. Such accusations should not be accepted at face value, however; upon closer examination, they appear to mask a stronger charge: that religion is not just irrational, subjective, and uncompromising, but inherently violent. This charge reflects the unspoken fear of public actors and institutions that failure to keep religion out of public life will result in the literal outbreak of religious war. The persistent influence of this mischaracterization of religion results from two misconceptions in current thinking about religion, secularism, and government.

The first stems from a failure to ask the right question—one cannot get the right answer from the wrong question. The relevant question on religious violence is not whether historically religion has been violent; obviously it has been. Rather, the question should be whether historically religion has been any more violent than secular ideologies; the answer to this question is not so obvious. Second, the conventional wisdom on church–state relations assumes that religion is a destabilizing antisocial force that can only be neutralized by a secular government which has complete sovereign authority over religion. While this is a more or less accurate summation of how Enlightenment thinkers conceived of the relationship of church and state, it does not reflect dramatic changes in both religion and government that have taken place in the centuries since.

In our view, the roles of church and state have reversed themselves over this period. The secular state is no longer necessary to protect society from the violence of religion allied with government, but religion now is necessary to protect society from the power and intrusion of the secular state. Thus, conventional American thinking on church and state relies on a remedy—exclusion of religion from public life—to correct a problem—religious violence—which now scarcely exists in the United States. Moreover, it does so at the cost of making all individuals in the United States more vulnerable to state domination. The final irony is that to the extent that religious violence remains a potential threat at all in contemporary American life, it is because of the alienation set in motion by the secularization of public life, and not because of anything inherent in the nature of contemporary American religion.

## A PARADOX

Undeniably, religion has spawned tremendous violence and conflict from the beginning of recorded history. Old Testament stories relate ancient Israel's wholesale slaughter of the preexisting inhabitants of Palestine. The ancient Greeks killed Socrates because he dared to question the existence and efficacy of their mythical gods. The pagans of Rome persecuted and enslaved the Christians who, following their rise to political power under Constantine, engaged in centuries of violence directed at Jews, Muslims, Protestants, and other "infidels." Prior to the advent of modern warfare in the 19th century, perhaps nothing matched the bloodshed and savagery of the Reformation wars. Despite having been settled by refugees from religious persecution in Europe, even colonial America burned witches and punished religious nonconformists.

The violence that has accompanied religion in history illustrates a paradox about societies influenced by religious belief. For the most part, the precepts of the major Western religions call for socially progressive actions by believers in their relations with each other and with nonbelievers, actions which we would judge desirable even by today's standards. The Golden Rule preached by Jesus in the New Testament—"love your neighbor as yourself,"[1] or "always treat others as you would like them to treat you"[2]—had long been a part of Jewish law,[3] and peace, tolerance, and reconciliation are fundamental Muslim beliefs.[4] Yet some of the most violent and socially regressive actions in history have been committed (and continue to be committed) by believers acting well within the mainstream of these religious traditions.

Denominational religion in particular has exhibited extraordinary creativity in fashioning justifications for persecution and violence directed at believers and nonbelievers alike, even when such actions appear to contradict the humanistic and progressive implications of orthodox beliefs. Christians in the colonial American South, for example, justified the enslavement and persecution of African Americans by stretching the interpretation of certain Old Testament texts. They concluded from these that Africans were descendants of Adam and Eve's son Cain, who was cursed by God for murdering his righteous brother Abel.[5]

By describing their slaves as inferior because of flawed ancestry, these purported followers of Jesus avoided the difficult task of reconciling their personal conduct with the Golden Rule. Because the slaves were thought less than human, it was not required to accord them equal respect as humans. Indeed, the theological absurdity of the "curse of Cain" permitted them to justify their un-Christian actions as nonetheless God's will.[6] Similarly justified religious violence persists in the Arab–Israeli conflict in the Middle East, the clash of Protestants and Catholics in Northern Ireland, the acts of Shiite extremists in Iran and elsewhere, and the fighting between Sikhs, Hindus, and Muslims in India.

Such examples are commonly cited as evidence of the inherently violent and oppressive nature of religion. We believe, however, that one cannot draw from these examples the conclusion that religion is by nature violent and oppressive. At least in the West, most of the historical violence associated with religion is more accurately characterized as stemming from the union of religious and government authority, rather than from some unique characteristic inherent in the nature of religion itself.

The violence of post-Reformation Christianity did not flow naturally from the words and commandments of Jesus, or from the doctrines of the medieval church as they had developed over the centuries, or from the theological implications of the Protestant dissent. Rather, the violence came from the imposition of a particular form of Christianity by threat of civil or criminal penalty. As we have observed, the very distinction of "religious" from "secular" was largely meaningless prior to the Reformation. Indeed, the distinction had been meaningless for over a thousand years, since the conversion of Constantine made Christianity the official religion of his declining empire. Kings and emperors ruled by the grace of God, and looked to alliances with the church—and in particular with its educated corps of priests and monks—as one way to control and expand their dominions.

Similarly, the church looked to civil rulers to expand the realm in which the church could safely impose its monopoly on access to God, and to protect the interests of the church in those kingdoms in which Christianity was already dominant. It did not hesitate to excommunicate those who failed to do its bidding, which constituted political as well as spiritual death in pre-Reformation times. Political sovereignty—the ultimate political power and authority in a country—did not rest exclusively with nations in the Middle Ages as it does today, but was shared with the church.

The same model was followed by many countries even in the early stages of the Reformation, such as the Lutheran principalities of northern Germany and Calvinist regimes in Switzerland. One simply cannot assess whether medieval and early Reformation religion was more or less violent than its host governments because until well after the Reformation they were intertwined.

One of the most important achievements of modern politics in the West was the separation of ecclesiastical power from civil authority. Nations no longer share their sovereign authority with churches and, accordingly, expulsion from a church no longer has significant legal or other civil consequences. If the violence historically associated with the pre-Reformation melding of ecclesiastical and civil authority stemmed solely or even primarily from religion, then one might have expected abatement of such violence once church and state were separated and religion legally subordinated to government. This, obviously, has not occurred.

The worst atrocities of the 20th century have been committed by secular regimes—Nazi Germany, Stalinist Russia, Maoist China, Khmer Rouge Cambodia. In contemporary Latin America, where the Roman Catholic church has been a progressive force at least as often as it has been a regressive one, violence and torture by governmental authorities have been common. The vicious reaction of "establishment" authorities to American civil rights and antiwar protestors in the 1960s—many of whom were from the religious left—proves that even governments with a substantial tradition of church–state separation are not immune from the temptation to use violence on their citizens. At the least, the ideologies that undergird and animate the secular state must share with religion the responsibility for continued war and violence in the contemporary world.

Despite the atrocities that have been committed on its watch, secular government has indispensable benefits in the modern world. It is hard to imagine that genuine religious freedom and other human rights would be available to religious dissenters living under a theocracy. Yet at the same time, the aggregation of political power that rests with the secular government of even liberal democracies represents a serious threat to individual freedom. The fact that the secular state can threaten as well as promote liberty does not negate the individual and social benefits that it generally provides in contemporary life.

We would suggest the same standard for assessing the contemporary importance and value of religion. Thus, we deny neither the historical violence of religion, nor the fact that such violence persists in the contemporary world. (We observe in passing, however, that most of the current examples of religious violence occur in contexts in which the separation of civil and ecclesiastical authority has commenced but is incomplete—civil authority in Northern Ireland clearly remains aligned with the Protestants; in Iran and other Arab nations, with Islam; in Israel with an increasingly orthodox Judaism; and in India, with Hinduism. More complete separation of ecclesiastical and state authority like that characteristic of most of Western Europe and North America might well lead to settlements of such conflicts or, at least, to reductions in the level of their violence.)

Our point is that there is nothing *uniquely* violent about religion, any more than there is anything uniquely pacifying about the secular state. Collective action of any kind—be it religious or secular—has the capability for destabilization and violence. Just as one must recognize the potential (and actual) oppression as well as the freedom made possible by modern liberal democracy, so also one must consider the benefits as well as the historical violence of religion. Only in this way can one fairly assess whether religion is justifiably excluded from American public life because of the violence historically associated with it.

## THE MISPERCEPTION OF RELIGIOUS VIOLENCE

Despite the fact that there does not appear to be anything uniquely violent about religion as compared to other forms of collective action, the Supreme Court periodically raises the specter of religious conflict and violence to justify excluding religion from American public life in all but its weakest and most diffuse forms. For example, in the first significant establishment clause case of the postwar era, *Everson v. Board of Education*, the Supreme Court considered whether a city could pay for bus transportation of school-age children to private and parochial as well as public schools. Along the way to holding that such funding was constitutionally permissible, the Court summarized what it saw as one of the historical forces behind the drafting of the establishment clause and its inclusion within the First Amendment:

The centuries immediately before and contemporaneous with the colonization of America had been filled with turmoil, civil strife, and persecutions, generated in large part by established sects determined to maintain their absolute political and religious supremacy. . . . In efforts to force loyalty to whatever religious group happened to be on top and in league with the government of a particular time and place, men and women had been fined, cast in jail, cruelly tortured, and killed.[7]

Observing that early American colonials had transplanted these violent religious practices to the New World, the Court stressed the insult and indignity of the fact that religious dissenters in America "were compelled to pay tithes and taxes to support government sponsored churches whose ministers preached inflammatory sermons designed to strengthen and consolidate the established faith by generating a burning hatred against dissenters."[8]

Relying on similar rhetoric, the Court in *Engel v. Vitale* suggested that the public school prayer at issue in that case carried the potential for the same persecution and violence that accompanied adoption of the Book of Common Prayer in 16th century England.[9] Again, in response to a 1968 Supreme Court decision which upheld state provision of textbooks to parochial school students, Justice Hugo Black, often identified as the intellectual leader of the Warren Court, flatly stated that "aid to religion and religious schools generates discord, disharmony, hatred, and strife among our people, and that any government that supplies such aids is to that extent a tyranny."[10]

Echoing this theme, the Court recently stated with respect to religion in *Edwards v. Aguillard* that "the public school is at once the symbol of our democracy and the most pervasive means for promoting our common destiny. In no activity of the State is it more vital to keep out divisive forces than in its schools."[11]

We have no quarrel with the Court's decisions banning public prayer and other such religious observances from the public schools. As much as we decry the absence of religion in American public life, we acknowledge that public schools are not appropriate sponsors of religious worship services. Nor do we quarrel with *Everson*'s and Justice Black's assessments of the evils of established religions.

We do challenge, however, the Court's superficial and uncritical analogies of contemporary church–state relations to those that existed centuries ago in Europe. One need not endorse public school prayer to recognize that comparing the controversy in *Engel* to the religious violence of post-Reformation Europe and post-Tudor England is over-stated, if not ridiculous. No one wants to relive the violence of the Reformation wars, but the real issue is whether the current political reality justifies this ominous rhetoric.[12]

This does not mean, of course, that religion is never violent or revolutionary. On the contrary, it often is. As we have argued, certain elements of the contemporary religious right have the potential for coalescing and evolving into such a force. This, however, is not because these elements are *religious*, but rather, because they are *excluded*. It is counterproductive from the standpoint of social and political stability to respond to these strident religious voices by working ever harder to silence them in public life. The unfortunate irony is that the possibility of revolt by American fundamentalists, however remote, becomes more rather than less likely when religion is persistently excluded from public life.

Despite the potential for religious revolt in the United States, an emphasis on the historical violence of religion distorts the character and contributions of American religion, because it has been a positive social influence as often as it has been a negative one. The abolitionist movements of the 19th century were centered in the northern Protestant churches, and the civil rights movements of the last generation drew strength and support from congregations of Protestants, Catholics, and Jews.

Contemporary peace issues, such as the sanctuary, gun control, and arms control movements, are strongly influenced by religious groups, in particular the mainline churches and other components of the Christian left. The American Catholic hierarchy has issued pastoral letters condemning war and economic injustice. These themes were given significant voice by (the Reverend) Jesse Jackson's 1988 campaign for the Democratic presidential nomination. Outside the United States, the mediation of violent political conflicts by clerics, as in Nicaragua and Poland, has become common in the last 10 years.

Certainly the United States in its two centuries of existence has seen nothing approaching the violence of the Reformation wars or the terrorism of any of the current religiously-based conflicts overseas. Religiously motivated violence in America, such as the Black Muslim separatist movements of the 1960s, and more recent instances of bombing and arson directed at abortion clinics, has never involved more than a minute segment of the religious population and has always been religiously idiosyncratic.

The clinic bombers operate at the very fringe of religious traditions whose orthodoxy offers no sanction for violent acts and rhetoric; it is clear that none of the denominations prominent in the prolife movement promise divine reward for those who murder prochoice people and destroy their property. A theology of violence simply does not naturally flow from the prolife movement. In fact, the most recent tactic adopted by those active in the movement has been nonviolent civil disobedience analogous to that advocated by Martin Luther King and other black civil rights advocates in the 1960s, much to the consternation of the prochoice movement.

Likewise, black separatism was motivated more by desires to reverse the dehumanizing effects of centuries of slavery and segregation than by the teachings of Islam, although the Muslim belief in *jihad* or "holy war" undeniably contributed to the movement's militancy and occasional violence, as it clearly contributes today to Palestinian terrorism.

On balance, however, the historical evidence does not support the proposition that religion in the modern world inevitably spawns conflict and violence. Accordingly, the conflict and violence that typify the modern world should not be laid at the door of religion. The overwhelming majority of Protestants, Catholics, Muslims, and Hindus neither participate in nor condone violence and terrorism. To blame these religions for the conflicts in Northern Ireland, the Middle East, and India is, therefore, simplistic and unfair. Catholicism has no more obligation to account for IRA terrorism than socialism has for Mussolini.

Those who insist on the exclusion of religion from public life on the basis of its violent, antisocial character are trapped in a shortsighted Enlightenment mode of thought that fails to appreciate that collective human action of any kind will often be intolerant and violent. More important, this mindset ignores that contemporary religion has evolved into a liberating and socially progressive force, while modern government has become more powerful, more intrusive, and more threatening to individual freedom.

## THE UNRECOGNIZED THREAT OF MODERN
## LIBERAL GOVERNMENT

A principal goal of the early liberal theorists was elimination and avoidance of the religious conflict and violence that had characterized the Reformation era. Having been traumatized by the Reformation wars, they remained deeply suspicious of the destabilizing potential of religious group action in the public arena.

Thomas Hobbes, for example, lived through the carnage and upheaval of the English Civil War during the 16th century, spending much of his life in exile under threat of persecution by Thomas Cromwell and the Puritan revolutionaries. It is not surprising that a central theme of his work—implicit in the titles of two of his most famous political works, *Leviathan* and *Behemoth*—is the need for a strong state sovereign to keep the peace among the various warring factions of religion. Hobbes thought even a despot was preferable to the carnage of civil war. Hobbes and other liberals sought to control what they saw as the violent and antisocial tendencies of religion by separating ecclesiastical authority from civil authority, thereby creating the distinction between the "religious" and the "secular."

As we discussed in Chapter 3, in the United States the influence of secularism eventually stripped religion of a public role and confined religious belief to the sphere of the private. As a matter of conscience, religious belief was placed beyond the regulatory reach of government. People were free to believe anything and everything they wished. In the realm of public action, however, religion was subordinated to government power. People could believe what they wanted, but once they sought to manifest those beliefs publicly through religious exercise and other actions, they became subject to government authority.

This fear of religion was shared by many people who lived during the founding era of the American republic. Some of these, in particular Thomas Jefferson and Thomas Paine, and to a lesser extent James Madison, feared the influence of collective religious action on government as much as the power of centralized government, a point sometimes lost on political and religious conservatives who plead for a return to the framers' understanding of the religion clauses. Indeed, the "original understanding" of the role of religion in American public life may not have been all that congenial to religion.

In a curious anticipation of the contemporary secularization hypothesis, some framers even saw denominational religion as an anachronistic superstition that would soon die out under the influence of the secular Enlightenment. For example, during the debate of the first House of Representatives over inclusion of the religion clauses in the proposed First Amendment to the Constitution, Congressman Thomas Scott noted that "it has been urged that religion is on the decline," and anticipated a time "when religion shall be discarded."[13]

Others of the framers were concerned about the unification of religion and centralized government, because they (correctly) saw such unification as inevitably leading to religious strife. James Madison saw religion as a source of factional conflict in politics. Thomas Jefferson, though not a participant in drafting or ratifying either the original Constitution or the Bill of Rights, likewise feared that failure to separate religion and government and to subordinate the church to the sovereign authority of the state would lead to the control of government by sectarian religion. This, in turn, could only end in violence as the sects sought to use government to coerce conformity to their beliefs and practices from believers and nonbelievers alike.

In the ensuing 200 or so years since the ratification of the Constitution and the Bill of Rights, government power at all levels—federal, state, and local—has grown beyond the wildest imaginations of even those framers who envisioned a strong central government. Large and important areas of modern life are subject to extensive government regulation, subsidization, or taxation.

Indeed, there is hardly any aspect of modern life that has not been touched by actual or attempted government supervision or control. The only areas that have remained somewhat free of this intrusion are those that fall within the relatively narrow enclaves protected by the Bill of Rights and other constitutional provisions, such as the First Amendment guarantees of free exercise of religion, speech, press, and assembly; the Fourth Amendment protections against unreasonable searches and seizures; and the Fourteenth Amendment protections of privacy and equality under the due process and equal protection clauses. Even these rights are not absolutely protected. In every case, the government retains the right to intrude upon constitutionally protected rights if it can show a "compelling government interest"—that is, if the government can show that its regulatory goal is so important that it properly may override even fundamental constitutional rights. And in the specific context of free exercise of religion, even this check has been eliminated. As we discussed in Chapter 5, in the current state of constitutional affairs, relatively unimportant government goals will justify even the destruction of religious culture and community.

Modern government has become nightmarish to deal with. Two hundred years ago in the world of the framers, citizens had personal access to the highest reaches of state and federal government as a resource to obtain redress for injustice. Even the president of the United States regularly received private citizens and heard their grievances until well after the Civil War. Modern government, however, has evolved into a vast, faceless, unaccountable bureaucracy that is controlled by no one and answers only to the forces of inertia. In the House of Representatives, which the framers expected to be the most democratically responsive arm of the federal government, the powers of incumbency now yield a reelection rate that exceeds that of the Soviet Politburo before perestroika. The difficulty faced by an individual citizen who must correct an error by the government or receive justice at its hands is perhaps the quintessential symbol of modern powerlessness.

The threat to liberty posed by modern government has its roots in the formulation of liberal political theory. The Enlightenment thinkers who were the authors of early liberal theory sought to separate government not only from religious authority, but from all moral conceptions of the good. Under a liberal government, matters of right and wrong are left to the individual to decide. Individuals have complete freedom to do whatever they please, so long as they do not harm others or threaten the authority of the state. The state, in turn, has as its principal responsibility maintenance of the civil peace, rather than the creation and maintenance of public values and morality.

Thus, one theoretical premise of liberal government is that such government must be neutral with respect to all conceptions of the moral good. Visions of right and wrong are pursued voluntarily by individuals and cannot be imposed, adopted, or encouraged by government. Serious issues are raised whenever the government engages in moral or value-creating enterprises in other than a neutral fashion.

To a large extent, the moral neutrality of government is an illusion. American government and the American constitution, as they have been interpreted by the Supreme Court, clearly prefer certain kinds of morality—such as, for example, individualism and relativism—over others. The important point here, however, is that under liberal political theory, government is not *supposed* to advocate any kind of morality. Accordingly, there is no unifying moral vision, no group of transcendent beliefs and values, to guide and inform the enterprise of modern government. Even more critical, there is no moral system to limit the reach of government. Modern American government is mostly about power and the extension of power.

Joseph Campbell tells the story of two American rugby players in the 1920s who perfected the forward pass. When they went over to England to play, however, their own teammates were uncomfortable with the pass even though it worked and asked them not to use the technique. "We don't play rugby that way, and we don't have rules for that sort of thing," they said. Campbell goes on to argue that the United States, as a radically pluralistic society, lacks the sort of shared ethic that characterizes a homogeneous society like England. We are bound together, Campbell says, not by shared morality, but rather by law. This is, perhaps, one explanation of why the United States is so litigious and legalistic.[14]

Unfortunately, the law that binds the United States together purports to be morally neutral, so that the lack of a shared moral vision in the United States extends far beyond leisure activities. Without any limiting visions of right and wrong, there are seemingly no boundaries on what government might do, no apparent limits to how far it might go in intruding upon the lives of individuals.

This lack of moral limits to government power that is inherent in liberal political theory becomes a frightening flaw when considered in light of the advances in science and technology that have characterized the 20th century. In earlier eras, even a government intent on domination could achieve it only to a limited extent. In preindustrial times, for example, the characteristic inefficiency of the bureaucracy and the difficulty of communication and travel provided some built-in protection of individual freedom even in regimes with repressive intentions.

George Orwell, however, visualized in *1984* what repressive government can do with the wonders of modern science. Historian A.D. Lindsay saw in Hitler's Third Reich Orwell's prophetic nightmare of the unrestricted power of modern government wedded to the wondrous efficiency of modern technology: "Is not Leviathan a parable of the impact of modern science on an unregenerate society? . . . Do we not read Hobbes with different eyes when we have seen Hitler and learnt how modern scientific development and modern technology can produce in reality Hobbes' Leviathan?"[15] Similarly, Paul Tillich observed that the Soviet Union under Stalin used "the most refined methods of the technical control of nature and society in order to maintain and increase its power. It use[d] terror in a way which never would have been possible without the triumph of technical reason in Western culture."[16]

Government in the United States, of course, has not begun to approach the repression and violence of Hitler's Germany or Stalin's Russia, and we do not mean to suggest otherwise. Still, the potential remains. Continued advances in computer technology enable the collection and storage of huge amounts of information on each citizen which can be easily retrieved by those who control the program. This has already occurred in public and private agencies that deal with tax collection, loan and other credit applications, and criminal law enforcement. Amazing progress in other technologies has led to the invention and use by law enforcement agencies of electronic surveillance equipment that can observe and record, accurately and undetected, the most private and intimate details of our lives. Continued improvement in nuclear, chemical, biological, and conventional weaponry makes our armed forces among the most knowledgeable and efficient in the world in the arts of inflicting pain, injury, and death. While we do not believe that the United States is poised to become a totalitarian state, we still think it wise to discard the comforting thought that totalitarianism and repression could never happen here. The possibility that they may be directed against religion in the first instance is no guarantee that they will not later be directed against all enterprises that challenge state authority. Totalitarian government tends not to be discriminate about whom it represses.

Having emerged from the political and social debris of the religious wars of the Reformation, the founders of the United States should be applauded for heeding the lessons of their history. Religion was indeed out of control, having become a tremendous force of social fragmentation and violence. It was essential to separate church and state, and to assert the sovereign control of government over religion. In modern America, respect for these principles eventually eliminated religious violence.

And therein lies the problem. The founders' concerns about religion are not ours. They feared uncontrolled religion at least as much as they feared unfettered government power, if not more so, because that is what their history had taught them to fear. But the United States of the 20th century is not post-Reformation Europe or post-Tudor England. We have never suffered from wars of belief, from the unification of government and denominational religious authority, or from the destructive fragmentation of our society along religious lines. We *have* suffered, however, and continue to suffer, from the effects of the inexorable expansion of the modern American liberal state. More ominously, each expansion of government jurisdiction and authority increases the threat that government poses to liberty in the United States.

## NOTES

1. Luke 10.25–27 (New English Bible).
2. Matt. 7.12 (New English Bible).
3. E.g., Lev. 19.34; 24.22 (New English Bible).
4. E.g., *The Qur'an: The First American Version*, trans. with comm. T. B. Irving (Brattleboro, Vt.: Amana, 1985), 22 (2.256, 2.263–64), 26 (3.19), 110 (10.100), 295 (49.9–10).
5. E.g., Genesis 4.1–15; 9.18–27 (New English Bible).
6. See Maddex, "A Paradox of Christian Amelioration: Proslavery Ideology and Church Ministries to Slaves" in *The Southern Enigma: Essays on Race, Class and Folk Culture*, ed. Walter J. Fraser, Jr. and Winfred B. Moore, Jr. (Westport, Conn.: Greenwood, 1983), 105.
7. 330 U.S. 1, 8–9 (1947).
8. Ibid., 10.

9. 370 U.S. 421, 425–33 (1962).

10. Board of Education v. Allen, 392 U.S. 236, 254 (1968) (dissenting opinion).

11. 482 U.S. 578, 584 (1987) (quoting McCollum v. Board of Education, 33 U.S., 203, 231 (1948) [opinion of Justice Felix Frankfurter]).

12. Cf. Gerard V. Bradley, "Dogmatomachy—A 'Privatization' Theory of the Religion Clause Cases," *St. Louis Law Journal* 30 (1986): 275, 308 ("No one wants the United States to become another Iran. But the real question is whether there is *any* warrant to suggesting that it might.") (emphasis in original).

13. Quoted in Daniel Farber and Suzanna Sherry, *A History of the American Constitution* (St. Paul, Minn.: West, 1990), 240.

14. Joseph Campbell, *The Power of Myth*, ed. Betty Sue Flowers (New York: Doubleday, 1988), 8–9.

15. A. D. Lindsay, *Religion, Science, and Society in the Modern World* (New Haven: Yale University Press, 1976), 21.

16. Paul Tillich, *Theology of Culture*, ed. Robert C. Kimball (New York: Oxford University Press, 1978), 185. See also ibid., 43–44.

# Chapter 10

# Beyond Perfectionism

Liberal political theory assumes that society is composed basically of two actors—the state and the individual. In fact, liberal societies have a third kind of actor—private associations and groups. These are important to individuals and to society for a variety of reasons. They help to preserve and to protect individual freedom, they provide supportive contexts for the development of individuality, and they are an important source of the values that are critical to self-government. In the United States, religious groups have historically performed all of these functions, and remain important because of the continuing commitment of large numbers of Americans to religious traditions. Yet the contributions of groups to society and to individuals, especially those of religious groups, entail their own costs.

American public life, with its emphasis on individuality and secularism, tends to emphasize these costs in the case of religious groups without taking full account of the related individual and social benefits that religion contributes. Rebutting the perfectionist critique entails the argument that one should not focus exclusively on the burdens of religion in contemporary American life to the exclusion of the individual and social benefits it provides. Religion is individually and socially valuable despite its imperfections.

It is painfully evident that religion has no adequate explanation for the hardships and oppression that have become routine in modern life. Indeed, religion bears responsibility for some of these events. However, science, philosophy, literature, and the other intellectual traditions of the

West also lack adequate accounts of these matters. Science in particular has helped many of them come to pass. Whatever its source, knowledge can be appropriated for good or ill.

The fact that religion is sometimes misused with unfortunate and even disastrous consequences should not invalidate it as a viable way of life in the contemporary world, any more than the misuse of technology to perpetrate violence and oppression should invalidate science as a means of gaining knowledge about the world. In both cases, one can work to eliminate distortions and perversions of the tradition while still recognizing its positive contributions to individual and social life.

## THE VALUE OF RELIGIOUS GROUPS

Religion is valuable to society and to individuals for at least three reasons. First, religious groups, along with other kinds of groups, protect the individual freedom of their members by providing an effective vehicle for challenging governmental power. Second, religious communities and traditions provide a context for the development of individuality and personality that is considered important by a substantial number of Americans. Finally, because liberal government is in theory constrained from both creating and advocating particular conceptions of morality, religious groups are part of the larger collection of necessary social institutions that create and maintain the values by which Americans choose to live their lives.

We argued in Chapter 9 that modern secular government poses a much greater threat to individual freedom than does contemporary religion. How does one counter the threat of the omni-powerful secular state? The pluralist thesis prevalent in American political thought argues that a large and diverse number of nongovernmental groups placed between the government and the individual is the best way of preserving individual liberty against government encroachment. Peter Berger and Richard Neuhaus have labeled such groups "mediating structures" because they act as buffers between individual citizens and the giant governmental and corporate bureaucracies that dominate contemporary society.[1] According to the pluralist thesis, mediating structures insulate the otherwise powerless individual against state coercion. Neighborhoods, families, unions, local schools, and (not least) churches and other religious groups fulfill this mediating function.[2] For example, the political role played by the Roman Catholic church during the 1980s in Poland, Nicaragua, and the Philippines demonstrated the extent to which a strong and assertive religious group can protect individual freedom from the repression of authoritarian and even totalitarian regimes. The institutional support and protection offered by the church to political dissenters in those countries are credited with shielding them from state retaliation for antigovernment activities.

Religion, then, is part of a larger group of voluntary, nongovernmental organizations which play an important role in the United States in empowering individuals to deal with the overwhelming coercion that is implicit in modern government. Strong, politically active religious groups are able to protect their members from domination by the government bureaucracies that have proliferated and intruded into virtually every aspect of contemporary life. Disabling religious groups from participating in public life leaves religious Americans, and indirectly all Americans, more vulnerable to government oppression.

Liberal political theory has generally conceived of communities and private associations as aggregations of individuals. Individuals constitute groups. It follows from this view that groups are entitled to no special protection by the legal system; such protection as they receive is derived from the rights of their individual members, and not from the status of the group *as a group*. Increasingly, however, it has been recognized that communities and groups give rise to many attributes of individualism, and not just vice versa. In other words, not only do individuals create groups, but, once formed, groups also create individuality. Law professor Ronald Garet argues that "groups and society are necessary conditions for the emergence of all that is morally valuable in individuality."[3] In particular, religious groups help the emergence and retention of individuality both by providing moral reference points against which their members can compare and contrast their moral assumptions and beliefs, and by supplying creative reinforcement and nurturing in the development of personality.

The critical relation of freedom of expression to self-realization and individual autonomy is a recurring theme of First Amendment jurisprudence. Expression of any sort, much less religious expression, does not take place in a social vacuum; there is always a community to which the expression is directed or referenced which gives the expression particular meaning and significance. "When we think about speech," writes Garet, "we imagine . . . a community of shared understanding, sustained communication, collective representations, and collective self-expression and self-understanding."[4] In expressing adherence or opposition to a set of values, an individual "takes a stand" and begins the process of defining and working out what she believes. This process of self-definition has a significant effect on a person—it makes her into a different personality than she would be in the absence of the effort to define her beliefs.

Religious groups can be important to the self-definitional process. Individuality is a social phenomenon rooted in one's relations with others. An individual's definition and sense of herself depends significantly on the nature of any recognition that is granted to her by others. Accordingly, a religious community that is committed to the autonomy, responsibility, and dignity of its members enhances the personality development of each by providing a vehicle for hearing, discussing, and ultimately accepting or rejecting transcendent religious ideals. To younger or newer members of a religious community, the values of the community are external and undiscovered. They must be taught and nurtured in the tradition by more experienced members.

As a member of a religious community matures in the tradition, she either gradually internalizes its religious values until they become part of her individual personality—"this is what I am"—or she rejects them—"this is what I am not." In either event, the religious community has played a significant role in her personality development.

Groups are sources of loyalty and solidarity, as well as references for personal growth. The support and reinforcement of some group of persons are critical to an individual's personal development. Ideally, each person should experience an environment of love, security, and acceptance, regardless of her failures and imperfections. Otherwise, individuals "are condemned to an impoverished and unfulfilled isolation."5 There are, of course, persons who succeed in resisting the influence of coercive and oppressive environments to become their own authentic personalities. As we have previously suggested, however, most people are made of lesser stuff.

In the face of an unrelenting secularism, many religious people will choose to marginalize or abandon their religious beliefs in order to earn the respect and support of dominant secular communities. People need a community, a group of others, to nurture them in their personality growth, to comfort them when things go poorly, to reinforce their choices and decisions, and to convey to them the essential message that they are valued and their presence would be missed.

Such acceptance enables an individual to define herself positively, to conclude that life is worth living even when she feels worthless. Viktor Frankl imagines that "someone looks down on each of us in difficult hours—a friend, a loved one, somebody alive or dead, or a God—and he would not expect us to disappoint him. He would hope to find us suffering proudly—not miserably—knowing how to die."6

As Frankl suggests, too often it is the lack of a nourishing and sustaining community that leads to apathy, depression, and suicide. For those numerous Americans who accept the values and beliefs of a religious community, the fellowship of that community can creatively and positively influence their personal development. The shared religious beliefs and experiences of the group give rich added meaning to the beliefs, experiences, and efforts of individual members of the community.

Since religious communities continue to be important sources of morality and self-definition for many Americans, hostility toward or ignorance of religious communities threatens to erode a critical context by which people arrive at their moral values and define the meaning of their existence. Curbing the public activity of religious groups thus strikes at the very heart of liberal philosophy—the preservation and promotion of individual autonomy, which ought to be one of the highest priorities of the liberal state.

Finally, groups are sources of moral values. As such, they make a critical contribution to the democratic process, and provide an additional, if indirect, check on the power of the modern secular state. This function, then, has both individual and social value.

In liberal society, the government has no competence to determine moral ends. Liberal government is formally without power to impose upon its people its view of what is "good" or "right"; it purports to be morally neutral, having only the power to keep the peace among its citizens and to protect their personal autonomy so that they can determine for themselves what is good or right. Morality in a liberal society originates outside of government, in the various choices and interactions among people in the private or nongovernmental sphere of society. In theory, then, the goals of liberal government depend on the moral values held by those that it governs. These goals are not shaped by any ethic internal to the state itself, but rather by the moral visions of the good society expressed by citizens through the political process.

These visions of the good, for the most part, originate and are maintained by group traditions, particularly religious ones. Most of the conceptual pillars of modern liberal democracy—impartial adjudication of disputes, judicial review of legislation, liability for negligent conduct, the presumption of innocence, habeas corpus, equality before the law, and good faith in the performance of contracts—have an origin or justification in the Judeo-Christian tradition.[7]

The very concept of equal respect for persons—perhaps the dominant theme of American constitutional law—grew out of ancient Israel's projection of its captivity in Egypt onto the rules of social coexistence in the promised land.[8] Religious groups, together with other group traditions, provide a pool of values and morality to individuals that liberal government theoretically is disabled from providing itself.

The moral values taught by religious and other group traditions serve an additional function in liberal society beyond creating and sustaining moral traditions that influence individuals and society. One danger of the moral neutrality of the modern secular state is that there is no internalized ethic to restrain the exercise of state power. The accomplishment of state goals becomes an end in itself, unconnected to any conception of right and wrong. The state, however, is not itself a living entity; it is composed of individuals who function together to accomplish its purposes. If these individuals have adopted a morality, that morality can serve as a restraint on the actions such individuals will take in pursuit of government goals. To the extent that religious and other group members participate in government, their group morality provides an internal restraint on the exercise of government power in addition to the external restraint represented by the political and social power of the groups themselves.

The life and growth of American society have been both enriched and protected by the contributions of religious groups. Cutting off this vast resource from American public life impoverishes society, depriving it of the enriching moral worldviews that religious groups contribute to American culture and politics and leaving it exposed to the amoral exercise of government power.

## THE THREAT OF RELIGIOUS GROUPS

Despite all of their individual and social contributions, the existence of groups, religious or otherwise, is not without its costs. First, the ability of groups to challenge the exercise of state power means that groups also threaten political and social stability. Group solidarity may encourage individual defiance of law. For example, the activities of the Roman Catholic Church in Poland, Nicaragua, and the Philippines, which we applauded for their protection of individual freedom, were also subversive, supporting those who wished to undermine the government. Since the regimes the church subverted were undemocratic and repressive, few could object to the church's antigovernment programs.

However, religious groups do not challenge only "bad" states. Contemporary political life is replete with examples of religious groups that represent regressive rather than progressive challenges to modern government. Liberal democracies, because they generally eschew repressive tactics, can only maintain order if most citizens obey and respect the law. Even a law that is generally obeyed may have to be amended or repealed if more than a very small minority consistently violates it. This prospect is troublesome for democratic government, whose premise is majority consensus. When a religious or other group challenges government power to regulate the group's actions and those of its members, it sows the seeds of lawlessness and rebellion.

Groups, moreover, are capable of imposing their own forms of repression on individuals. Though groups protect individual freedom from encroachment by government, they also erode that same freedom by the manner in which they admit, control, and expel their members. Those who do not conform to the basic beliefs and behavioral standards of a group will be expelled or ostracized because of failure to conform to the group orthodoxy. Because a significant portion of an individual's identity often is tied to identification and interaction with a group, the threat of expulsion or disapproval is serious. Faced with the prospect of losing fellowship with those who shape her life, the group member understandably feels severe pressure on her freedom to choose.

This infringement on personal choice is prevalent in religious groups, especially hierarchical and conservative ones. By their nature, religions are not neutral about the best way to live one's life, and religious communities commonly reject those who do not accept their basic values. Beliefs and actions that violate the wisdom of a religious tradition are condemned as wrong and, if the violations are sufficiently serious, result in excommunication.

Though it champions individual freedom in many parts of the world, the Roman Catholic church is frequently criticized by Americans for the restrictions that it attempts to impose on its members on a wide range of moral and social issues, such as abortion, birth control, divorce, premarital sex, and the ordination of women to the priesthood. Sometimes failure to conform is accompanied by sanctions short of outright excommunication, such as denial of the sacraments, expulsion or suspension from a religious order, or revocation of a theological license.

For the person who has grown up committed to the Catholic community and defined by reference to its culture and traditions, punishment and rejection by the main body of the church verges on personality destruction. A nonconforming Catholic may be forced to choose between her moral beliefs and the very community that defines herself and gives those beliefs meaning. The coercion implicit in such a choice is obvious.

Finally, just as religious groups do not challenge only repressive governments, so also the moralities preserved by religious groups as influences on society are not always desirable ones. Similarly, although morality may be a check on the amoral exercise of government power, it may also appropriate government power to its own ends.

Thus, the individual freedom that is protected and preserved by a vigorous plurality of groups in American society comes at the cost of threats to governmental stability and the freedom of those individuals whose behavior and beliefs do not conform to the norms of politically and socially important groups. Individuals experience personal freedom in a pluralistic society only to the extent that their individuality is consistent with the norms dictated by the group or groups to which they belong or with which they identify themselves. Those who find themselves at odds with those groups which have provided a reference for self-identification and development will be more isolated and vulnerable than ever.

## THE NECESSITY OF RELIGIOUS GROUPS

Despite their negative attributes, groups are a social and political necessity in modern life. Some of our most cherished individual rights, such as freedom of speech, freedom of association, and free exercise of religion, have their roots in the support and solidarity of group action. If one is genuinely concerned about threats to individual freedom, the pertinent question is whether we now have more to fear from unlimited government power than we do from the coercion implicit in religious group membership.

As we have argued, whatever the dangers to liberty that once were presented by religion and its capacity for repression and violence, these today are outweighed by the capacity for repression and violence that is wielded by the secular state. Individuals can always leave a religious group, difficult as that may be, but they cannot escape the reach of state power. Continued insistence on confining religion to the narrow sphere of the private in order to avoid conflict and violence directs our attention and resources towards solving a problem that no longer exists in the United States.

Moreover, it renders us vulnerable to a far greater threat that has steadily grown with the expansion of government—that of dominance by the secular state—by undermining the power of religious groups to challenge state authority. Thus, the demise of religion and religious groups would put even the liberty of nonbelievers at risk. Vital and active religious groups, among others, are a democracy's best insurance against such domination.

Accordingly, the unreflective Enlightenment charge that religion is inherently violent should hardly count as a criterion for evaluating religion. On the contrary, not only is religion not inherently violent, it is essential to the preservation of individual freedom in the United States, which recommends it as a participant in American public life.

Just as important, religion and religious communities provide the context for the development of personality and individuality of religious Americans. Excluding religion from public life strips religious people of their identities whenever they attempt to participate in public contexts. Although it is true, as we have suggested, that religious groups can coerce and repress individuals, the extent to which this occurs in a given case can be an extremely complicated question. Group restrictions on individual freedom and choice in the short run may be designed to enhance freedom in the long run.

Many religious traditions in particular believe that the achievement of authentic human happiness lies in a life lived in conformity to demanding standards of personal conduct. Thus, what may appear to be group coercion of individual choice may in actuality be the individual's decision to find lasting personal fulfillment by denying herself transitory desires and wants. If individual autonomy is truly at the heart of liberalism, then to be true to its own premises, liberalism must accommodate religious belief in public life.

For these reasons, a large number of diverse and vigorous nongovernmental groups, including religious groups, is deemed essential in American society despite their individual and social costs:[9] "While in liberal *theory* the community value is anti-individualistic, it has always been recognized in liberal *practice* that protection of individualistic rights, whether against other individuals acting alone or in collectivities up to and including the state, can often be achieved only through communities other than the state itself."[10]

Religion, like so much else in human existence, is a mixture of good and evil. There are always negatives to balance against the positives. Our argument is that, despite its negatives, there is so much good that is accomplished by religion on both an individual and a social level that the negatives are worth enduring. Retaining religion as a vital part of our national culture—one part of "choosing the dream"—reflects the view that, on balance, legitimizing a public role for religion leads to a better national life than would privatizing or eliminating it.

In the modern era, the tendency has been to allow the negative attributes of religion to eclipse its positives. To continue to view religion in this manner is unwarranted. For example, the economic and other abuses committed in the name of capitalism are legion in American and world history, from the robber barons of the 19th century to the environmental atrocities committed by contemporary multinational corporations. Does this mean that capitalism is an unmitigated evil, and that private corporations and capital should be banned? To do so would be unfortunate; we have recently learned through example after example that political freedom and economic freedom are correlated.

In Korea, China, the Soviet Union, and the Eastern bloc countries, both people and governments are discovering that private capital formation and market price mechanisms generate pressures for political freedom; conversely, political reforms tend to make citizens unwilling to undergo the shortages, unemployment, and other economic hardships and inefficiencies that inevitably accompany economies in which goods and services are allocated by nonmarket devices such as centralized planning. The contemporary challenge is not to abolish capitalism, but to preserve free markets and private capital in an effective form while mitigating the hardships that seem to be the byproduct of capitalist economies.

A similar example is found in modern science. Some of the most horrible atrocities of the modern age would have been impossible without the advances in sophisticated weaponry provided to the world by scientists. The Holocaust of World War II is perhaps the deepest and darkest scar on the face of Western history. Eleven million people, including fully one-third of all the Jews of Europe, were systematically exterminated by Nazi Germany. The roots of the Holocaust are complex, but there can be no doubt that it was made possible in part by a macabre marriage of scientific innovation to anti-Semitism. More recently, the uncovering of the secrets of the subatomic world by modern physicists resulted in the development of the nuclear weapons, with their capacity literally to destroy the world.

Again, it hardly follows from these perversions of science that science itself is an unredeemable evil which must be banished for the protection of human life. The advances in scientific knowledge of the past century have resulted in enormous increases in the standard of living all over the world, and have greatly increased our understanding of human life and its place in the universe. Our lives would be diminished without this knowledge.

The challenge of contemporary science is to keep continually in view its own limitations. Science can tell us *how* do to almost anything, once we decide what it is we want to do; what science cannot do is tell us *what* it is that we ought to do in order to live rich and authentic human lives.

We must continue to accept the advances in knowledge that science offers, while straining to control the use of that knowledge for evil. To date, no one has suggested that to lessen the magnitude of the task, we eliminate science altogether.

One who catalogues the sins of religion must take account of its virtues. It is true that religion can be violent and oppressive. It is also true that religions often forget that their mission is "not of this world," as they go lusting after worldly power and ambition and leave undone the more crucial tasks of ministering to the needs of their members. Lastly, it is true that, despite their claims, religions do not hold all of the answers to important human dilemmas.

But, at the same time, religion can bring peace, to nations and to individuals. It protects its members from oppression even as it may oppress them itself. Moreover, ministry is not a wholly private function; witnessing to the world against suffering and injustice is the most public of acts, and one that religion has frequently performed in American history. And finally, if it must be conceded that many of the perplexing issues of human existence are not satisfactorily dealt with by religion, it must also be admitted that these issues are not definitively answered by science, philosophy, literature, or any of the secular disciplines, either. As we would not wish to do without any of these disciplines in our search for answers, so also we should not wish to do without religion.

## NOTES

1. Peter L. Berger and Richard John Neuhaus, *To Empower People: The Role of Mediating Structures in Public Policy* (Washington, D.C.: American Enterprise Institute, 1977), 2–3.

2. Ibid., 8–40; Bruce Hafen, "Developing Student Expression Through Institutional Authority: Public Schools as Mediating Structures," *Ohio State Law Journal* 48 (1987): 663; Staughton Lynd, "Communal Rights," *Texas Law Review* 62 (1984): 1417.

3. Ronald Garet, "Communality and Existence: The Rights of Groups," *Southern California Law Review* 56 (1983): 1002, 1044.

4. Ibid., 1023.

5. Alan Hutchinson and Patrick Monahan, "Law, Politics, and the Critical Legal Scholars: The Unfolding Drama of American Legal Thought," *Stanford Law Review* 36 (1984): 199, 239 n.179.

6. Viktor Frankl, *Man's Search for Meaning: An Introduction to Logotherapy*, trans. Ilse Lasch (Boston: Beacon, 1959), 132.

7. See Harold Berman, *The Interaction of Law and Religion* (Nashville, Tenn.: Abingdon, 1974), 71, 94–95, 103–104.

8. Cynthia Ozick, "The Moral Necessity of Metaphor," *Harper's Magazine* 272, (May 1986): 62, 67.

9. Professor Gedicks has developed this theme at length in "Toward a Constitutional Jurisprudence of Religious Group Rights," *Wisconsin Law Review* 1989: 99.

10. Ian Macneil, "Bureaucracy, Liberalism, and Community—American Style," *Northwestern University Law Review* 79 (1985): 900, 900 n.5 (emphasis in original).

*Chapter 11*

# Beyond Secularism

The last three chapters have laid the groundwork for a reorientation of religion and public life, rebutting common justifications for privatizing religion and religious experience and excluding them from public life. Religion is neither objective nor wholly rational; neither, however, is most secular knowledge. Religion has at times been a violent and oppressive force in Western history; however, the secular state has been violent and oppressive as well, notwithstanding its separation from ecclesiastical authority. Indeed, at this juncture in the history of the United States, government almost certainly represents a greater threat to individual freedom than religion does. Finally, despite its common flaws, religion at its best makes immeasurable, positive individual and social contributions in contemporary America.

At this point, we wish to sketch what public life might look like if religion were admitted as a full and equal participant. What does religion have to offer to American public life? Ultimately, it is only the positive vision of a society in which religion is naturally part of public life and culture that can convince people to discard a secularized public life.

## REPLACING THE SEPARATIONIST METAPHOR

We have argued that the privatization of religion that comes with secularizing American public life encourages the abandonment, the neutralization, and (potentially) the revolt of religion. None of these is desirable. Elimination of religion as a significant influence on human behavior might be celebrated in some quarters. As we discussed in Chapter 10, however, it would deprive many Americans of the reference point by which they define themselves and their lives, at the same time that it would deprive society of the many socially valuable functions that religious organizations currently perform. Most important, with the elimination of such a large group of institutions that mediate between government and individuals would also come increased individual vulnerability to state domination and oppression.

These unhappy alternatives are forced upon us by a habit of thinking which separates religion and religious experience from American public life. Separatist thinking requires that the church be rigorously separated from the state in order to avoid religious warfare of the type that plagued Europe in earlier centuries and that continues to some extent even today. Religion must be kept private, it is believed, because it is neither rational nor empirical nor objective, making it impossible to talk about in public contexts. As a mere taste or preference, it is beyond political analysis in the liberal scheme of things. Finally, religion is held to impossibly high standards, being condemned for its failings and weaknesses without receiving credit for the strengths and benefits it contributes to individuals and to society. If separation, secularization, and privatization result in the demise of religion, the assumption of public culture seems to be that other (secular) groups could take over its functions.

We have attempted to show that these habitual ways of thinking about church–state relations are flawed. Whatever may have been the situation in the United States two centuries ago, the rigorous separation of church and state that has been enforced by the Supreme Court since World War II is simply not necessary to keep the religious peace today. Moreover, by eviscerating religious institutions, such separation threatens to leave us more vulnerable to the ever-expanding power of government. Certain elements of religious belief and experience are certainly nonrational, but other parts of them are rational and subject to scientific inquiry. At the same time, modern science is neither so rational nor so objective as we are accustomed to thinking. Religion should not be discarded for its flaws and mistakes any more than capitalism or science should be abandoned for theirs; so long as it contributes significantly to our individual and social well-being, we should work to reform it, not to eliminate it.

The conceptualization of religion in American life must be altered. Religion should not be regarded as a dangerous virus to be walled off and confined to private life, but as a full and valuable participant in public life. The "wall of separation" made famous by Thomas Jefferson is a misleading metaphor for the relationship of church and state in the contemporary United States. The oppositional dualisms of secular versus religious, church versus state, and public versus private implied by the separation metaphor force one into a confrontational mode in thinking about religion in public life. This metaphor and these dualisms ought to be abandoned. They encourage talk about "religion *and* politics," as if the two defined separate and mutually exclusive realms.

Instead, public culture must rediscover that, at least in the United States, religion is one of the influences that *creates* politics. What many Americans want from their government and their country derives from their religious beliefs. What public culture needs are ways of talking about religion and politics, church and state, and public and private life which unify rather than divide. Indeed, what we need first of all is a way for the religious and the secular to talk to each other.

Argument, Milner Ball has written, is ultimately a communal act which implies respect for the other participants without conceding the points of contention. "When we engage in argument, persuading and being persuaded, we practice mutual dignity. The other person must be convinced; the other deserves to be convinced."[1]

The first step in granting religion a place in public life is granting that it has a legitimate role to play there. We described how religion now is admitted to the public square only grudgingly, if it is perceived to wield significant political power. Thus, religion is admitted only as an interest group. If, as we have argued, religion *as religion* is allowed to enter into the conversations about important issues that are carried on in American public life, then it becomes recognized as having something to say about those issues whose merits the other participants in public life should consider in their deliberations. The knowledge that the religious voice is being heard—acknowledged as being worthy of being listened to, even if not agreed with—greatly reduces the alienation that a secularized public life will otherwise produce. Because they know that public culture hears and even values their views, religious people regain a stake in participating within the system.

The replacement metaphor we would propose, then, is the metaphor of conversation. Professor Ball, for example, has suggested that the law should be viewed as a communicative medium, a way of talking to others about complex issues, rather than as a wall or bulwark against bad consequences.[2] Similarly, Michael Perry has argued that the principal purpose of constitutional law is to facilitate moral dialogue, arguing that such dialogue is possible even in a society whose members do not share identical moralities.[3] Dialogue is not only possible, he suggests, but highly desirable, because it almost always transforms society for the better.

In our view, then, the ideal relation between religion and public life—the religious and the secular—is one that ensures that all voices are heard with seriousness and respect. Again, in a truly postmodern society, no discourse can be privileged and no discourse disabled in public life. "Civil conversation" can be the beginning of a reconciliation between religion and public life.

## DEVELOPING A PUBLIC RELIGIOUS LANGUAGE

Separation metaphors will not easily be replaced by conversation metaphors. Before the secular and the religious can converse, they require a common language, and this the United States does not have. Americans share a common tongue (more or less), but by "language" we mean more than this. Language is culture: how we talk about ourselves is one of the ways that we define who we are as a people. Every language is adapted to the ideas, and needs, and experiences of the people who use it.

For example, consider the language of a native American tribe that lives at the edge of the polar ice cap. Living in the harshness of a virtually perpetual winter, these tribal dialects have numerous words describing an almost infinite number of gradations of cold and snow. They have only one word for "hot," however, which takes in everything from lukewarm to boiling. Compare this with the dialects of tribes that live in the tropical rainforests of Central and South America. There words reflect almost the opposite—many words for concepts and ideas of heat, and only a very few, imprecise words for communicating concepts and ideas of cold.[4]

Each tribe's language reflects its unique experiences and needs, and understandably fails to reflect experiences and needs that they do not have. Any attempt to translate concepts of cold into a rainforest dialect, or concepts of heat into an Arctic dialect, is bound to be imprecise, if not impossible. The words simply are not there.

An interesting statement of the problem is contained in a passage from Nikos Kazantzakis's controversial novel, *The Last Temptation of Christ*. The passage is based on a New Testament story which recounts that a Roman centurion sought out Jesus and asked him to heal a beloved and mortally afflicted servant.[5] Jesus performed the miracle, and the servant recovered. In the novel, Kazantzakis imagines Jesus and the centurion to have had a subsequent encounter. After reiterating his gratitude to Jesus for having healed the servant, the centurion finds that he has little else to say. Like most Romans, he despises Jews as uncivilized; he is baffled that someone as powerful and gifted as Jesus would be at home in Jewish culture:

"How can you talk to this pack of dogs?" the centurion asked.

Jesus blushed. "They are not dogs," he said, "but souls, sparks of God. God is a conflagration, centurion, and each soul a spark to be revered by you."

"I am a Roman," answered [the centurion], "and my God is a Roman. He opens roads, builds barracks, brings water to cities, arms himself in bronze and goes to war. He leads, we follow. The body and soul you talk of are one and the same to us, and above them is the seal of Rome. When we die both soul and body die together—but our sons remain. That is what we mean by immortality. I'm sorry, but what you say about the kingdoms of heaven seems just a fairy tale to us."

After a pause, he continued: "We Romans are made to govern men, and men are not governed by love."

"Love is not unarmed," said Jesus. . . . "Love too makes war and runs to the assault."

"It isn't love, then," said the centurion.

Jesus lowered his head. I must find new wineskins, he reflected, if I'm to pour in new wine. New wineskins, new words. . . .6

The centurion's conception of human life as being devoid of spiritual dimensions and dominated by the exercise of power stood in such stark contrast to Jesus's teachings that "love" in the Christian sense had no meaning for him; he simply could not understand it. Another word would have had to be appropriated or invented for genuine dialogue to take place.

As things now stand in American public life, religious concepts spoken in public contexts must be referenced to secular culture. That is, religion must speak in the language of secularism. As we have discussed, however, religious belief and experience do not easily translate into secular language. "The person who has had a mystical experience knows that all the symbolic expressions of it are faulty," declares Joseph Campbell. "The symbols don't render the experience, they suggest it. If you haven't had the experience, how can you know what it is?"7

The idea of God talking to humanity is simply alien to a humanistic worldview that is highly influenced by rationality, objectivity, and empiricism. What is needed is a language that can begin to capture the nature of religious experience, but that is still understandable by secular culture. How is the United States to develop such a language?

### Religion and Public Education

First, one of the reasons why the assertion of religious beliefs and experiences in public seems so strange and inappropriate is that since World War II, American children have stopped learning about religion and participating in religious activities in public schools. As we have discussed, the expulsion of religion from public elementary and secondary schools is virtually complete. The goal of the Enlightenment was the overthrow of religious superstition in favor of reason, education, and science as the means of gaining knowledge about the world. This hallmark of Enlightenment thinking—the privileging of secular styles of discourse like rationalism and objectivity—continues to undergird the Supreme Court's decisions on religion in public schools. It clearly is the basis of one of the Court's latest pronouncements on the issue of religion in public schools, *Edwards v. Aguillard*.[8]

In *Edwards*, the Court considered the constitutionality of Louisiana's "Balanced Treatment Act," which prescribed the teaching of "creation science" in public school science courses whenever the theory of evolution was also taught. Creation science is a recent attempt by conservative religion to account for the origin of human beings in a way that is both scientific and consistent with the account of human creation in the Old Testament. (However, Christian fundamentalists are not the only ones who have objected to the installment of secularism as the privileged discourse on human origin in American public education.[9]) The Court concluded that the Act violated the establishment clause.

Beginning its analysis by noting the traditional antagonisms between evolution and conservative religious beliefs about the origin of human life, the Court then determined that creation science entailed belief in a supernatural creator. From there, the Court found it an easy step to conclude that the Act's principal—and constitutionally impermissible—purpose "was to change the science curriculum of public schools in order to provide persuasive advantage to a particular religious doctrine that rejects the factual basis of evolution in its entirety."[10]

Oddly, it is clear that the Act did not seek to privilege creation science in the public school discussion about human origins; it sought merely to grant it entrance to the curriculum. According to the Court, however, if one is going to talk about human origins in public schools, religion is an unacceptable language in which to do so. One talks in the secular language of science, or not at all. As Justice Scalia pointed out in his dissenting opinion, the Court's opinion betrayed an intellectual predisposition created by the facts and the legend of *Scopes v. State*—an instinctive reaction that any governmentally imposed requirements bearing upon the teaching of evolution must be a manifestation of Christian fundamentalist repression.[11]

By now, secularism is well-established as the discourse privileged to be admitted to public schools, and its privilege is exclusive.

Religion has been one of the dominant influences in the development of Western civilization, for both good and ill. It continues to be important in American and international affairs. It lies at the heart of everyday life for many Americans, and continues to be a source of both inspiration and conflict in the United States. Failing to teach about religion in history and in contemporary society is, quite simply, a failure of public education. Moreover, as we have discussed, it is oppressive to religious people to act as if they and their religion do not exist. Finally, treating religious people as if they have some intellectual disease which threatens to infect the entire population, as did the Supreme Court in *Edwards*, is insulting.

Fortunately, numerous educational and nonsectarian groups have recognized this failing. Teaching and educational support groups have begun to advocate that public schools explicitly teach about American and world religions. We emphasize, as these groups have emphasized, that the goal is to teach *about* religion and to permit equal access to school facilities by voluntary student religious groups. The public schools, with their compulsory attendance policies and public funding, should not be converted into vehicles of sectarian indoctrination. Neither, however, should they be permitted to remain vehicles of secular indoctrination. By recognizing religion and religious people as normal components of history and contemporary life, the public schools could facilitate creation of a language which incorporates and presupposes the legitimacy of religious participation in American public life.

### Religion and Public Policy

Another way to develop a language for religious–secular dialogue is suggested by another recent Supreme Court case, *Bowen v. Kendrick*.[12] In *Bowen*, the Court considered a challenge to the constitutionality of the Adolescent Family Life Act, which permitted religious groups, among other social service groups, to receive funds for services and research relating to adolescent pregnancy and sexual activity. The Court held that the Act, as it was written by Congress, did not violate the establishment clause even though it permitted the channeling of public funds to religious organizations.

Pregnancy and sexual activity among teenagers are widely regarded as a serious national problem, if not an outright crisis. There seems to be general agreement that teen promiscuity in general and teenaged parents in particular are not desirable. A variety of ways of helping teenagers to avoid or to mitigate the risks of early sexual activity and pregnancy have been suggested over the last decade, including better sex education, wider distribution of contraceptives, and less expensive and more accessible abortion procedures. Various counseling methods also attempt to dissuade teens from being sexually active (or, at least, from engaging in indiscriminate sex) by emphasizing that adolescents are unprepared and incapable of properly dealing with the complex psychological, social, financial, and other difficulties and commitments associated with sexual activity, childbearing, and parenting.

One can advocate any or all of these approaches without having to take any moral or religious position on whether it is right or wrong for teenagers to be sexually active and to bear and raise children. Indeed, this is thought to be one of their virtues by those who believe that teenagers are not influenced in their sexual behavior by prudish advice about abstinence. Yet lack of morality is the flaw in these approaches, not their strength. They suffer from the infirmity common to all attempts to teach moral behavior without reference to a definitive moral standard. They appeal principally to the self-interest of teenagers, rather than attempting to teach them what is right. The hope is that teens will be persuaded that it is simply not prudent to have children or to be sexually active at their age.

This approach strongly resonates with the liberal conception of the autonomous individual. Under liberalism, an individual is assumed to have a legitimate interest in satisfying her preferences, wants, and desires. In other words, what someone wants, someone ought to get, as long as it harms no one else. Liberal government itself, as we have noted, purports to be morally neutral. As an autonomous individual, the teenager who is unpersuaded by prudential arguments about abstinence has a legitimate interest—one that a morally neutral liberal government is bound to respect—in being sexually active and in bearing and raising children.

Appeals to self-interest that are inconsistent with one's preferences, wants, or desires are not usually very effective in teaching morality. The moral life is never the way of least resistance. This is especially the case when dealing with adolescent sex. It requires considerable wisdom and maturity to project the consequences of a decision about sexual activity or pregnancy into one's future and decide to forego immediate sexual gratification, and adolescents are not known for either wisdom or maturity.

Not surprisingly, studies show that education alone is ineffective in deterring teens from engaging in sexual activity.[13] Teenagers remain remarkably naive about sex, childbearing, and childrearing despite significant efforts at sex education. They tend to make decisions in this area with their hormones, not with their heads. And certainly the general liberal assumption that one's legitimate interests coincide with one's sexual, emotional, and other desires gives adolescents little reason to forego immediate sexual gratification.

Liberalism is not the only vantage point from which to analyze this problem. We offered in Chapter 8 the concept of "flourishing" as a way in which to judge the individual and social value of religious experience. Michael Perry has argued that one only has a legitimate interest in satisfying those preferences, wants, and desires that lead to one's flourishing—that lead to one's living the most satisfying life of which she is capable, given the religious or other moral tradition to which she subscribes. He admits that there is not likely to be consensus on precisely what kind of life leads to one's flourishing. He does argue, however, that there is often societal consensus on the sorts of moral systems that do *not* lead to flourishing.

The apartheid of the pre–civil rights South, for example, not only enslaved African Americans, but also stunted the moral growth and progress of white society. Thus, merely to have a desire does not mean that one has a legitimate interest in satisfying it, if it is not likely to lead to her flourishing.[14] Sometimes people want things that are not good, for them or for anyone else. It is the job of the moral educator to help them to understand this. Placing a moral principle within the context of a religious or other moral tradition enables one to teach far more powerfully than is possible with prudential argument. It enables one to teach, for example, that adolescent pregnancy is wrong, not just ill-advised.

A recent panel discussion at the University of Michigan illustrates our point. The subject was the proper role of religion in the public schools. One panelist stated his difficulty with a schoolteacher's identifying behavior as "immoral"; the limit of the teacher's authority, in this panelist's view, was the right to label the behavior "inappropriate." This position was attacked by a rabbi on the panel as "an inability to take a moral stand."[15] The rabbi was right.

How can one expect a child to make moral choices at the expense of her own wants and desires without being willing to teach the child that the relevant considerations extend beyond self-gratification and propriety? Placing a moral principle in the context of a tradition, religious or otherwise, gives the principle a compellingness and force that dwarf mere appeals to personal expedience and social convention. At a minimum, this kind of context enriches the whole idea of self-interest by deepening one's understanding of oneself and one's moral beliefs.

The *Bowen* Court's rejection of the initial constitutional challenge to the Adolescent Family Life Act was wise. So long as there is no coercion or deception, government should be free financially to assist religious groups as part of a general social program when the group's religious teachings are consistent with governmental policy goals. In the absence of coercion or deception, it would seem that a child who is thought sufficiently mature to choose voluntarily to have sex, to bear a child, and to become a parent also is capable of deciding that her interests are best served by seeking religious counseling on these matters.

Failure to fund religious counseling equally with nonreligious counseling removes the religious voice from the conversation about individual and social solutions to questions of teenage sexual activity, and privileges voices that reflect secular morality or no morality. By contrast, the consistent interaction of government and religion in a public context like that created by the Act can help to develop a public culture in which religion is acknowledged and assumed to have something worthwhile to contribute to the debate on this issue—once again, the beginning of a language and a dialogue between religion and secularism.

### Religion and Oppressive Legislation

Granting equal status to religion as a participant in public life implies that religion is a worthwhile activity—at least one as worthwhile as numerous secular activities whose sponsors already enjoy presumptive acceptability in American public life. As a socially and individually valuable enterprise, religion would seem to merit some sort of protection from the threats that inhere in an era of greatly expanded government, in the same way that political parties and the media are protected. Religion simply cannot be effective in doing those things which make it socially and individually valuable unless it is relatively free.

And religion cannot be relatively free in a country in which government regulates, subsidizes, or taxes virtually every aspect of life unless affirmative action is taken to create nongovernmental space in which religion (and other nongovernmental activities) can grow and flourish. The Supreme Court, Congress, and the state legislatures must commit themselves to a constitutional doctrine of free exercise of religion that is meaningful, in contrast to the narrow and dishonest "protection" it affords to religion today.

Current Supreme Court holdings offer virtually no protection to the individual or group whose religious conscience conflicts with generally applicable law. If there were any doubts about this, they were laid to rest by the Court's most recent free exercise decision, *Employment Division v. Smith*.[16] In *Smith*, two native Americans who worked for a private drug rehabilitation clinic were fired because they used the hallucinogenic drug peyote in connection with certain sacramental rituals of the Native American Church. In addition to losing their jobs, they also were denied unemployment compensation on the ground that even religious use of peyote was prohibited by state law.

The evidence at the trial showed that use of peyote was a 300-year-old tradition of the Native American Church, that its use was carefully controlled by the church and rarely abused, and that the occasional sacramental use of the drug by the church did not lead to addiction. (In fact, studies have shown that the peyote rituals of the Native American Church are highly effective in combatting alcoholism among native Americans, because they promote self-esteem and encourage abstention from alcohol consumption.) Finally, it was clear that the native Americans could not fully practice their religion without occasional use of peyote. Nevertheless, the state refused to grant the native Americans a religious exemption from the regulations that denied them unemployment benefits.

On appeal, the Supreme Court held that even though use of peyote was required by the native Americans' religion, the state was not constitutionally required under the free exercise clause to exempt them from the regulations which denied them benefits. Moreover, the Court held that the state did not even need to articulate an important reason for withholding benefits. In the Court's view, American society "cannot afford the luxury of deeming *presumptively invalid*, as applied to the religious objector, every regulation of conduct that does not protect an interest of the highest order."[17] In other words, the government may engage in regulation that effectively prohibits the free exercise of a religion without even having to identify an important goal or policy that is served by the regulation. This is tantamount to holding that if Prohibition-era laws had not exempted the sacramental use of wine, the free exercise clause would not have protected Catholics and Protestants

from criminal prosecution or civil penalties for participating in communion services.

It is one thing to burden religion for a good reason; *Smith*, however,
suggests that government may burden religion for even a trivial one. As
the dissenting opinion points out, careful review of government action
which burdens the free exercise of one's religion is hardly a " 'luxury,'
but an essential element of liberty specifically protected by the First
Amendment."[18] One can only imagine the bitterness and anger among
native Americans whose most sacred religious rituals have been labeled
excesses that the United States can do without.

The majority in *Smith* suggested that exemptions from generally
applicable law should be written, if at all, by the legislature or Congress
that enacts such law.[19] Legislative and Congressional exemptions are
not uncommon, but they are not universal, as the Court's own precedents evidence. As we related in Chapter 5, numerous state and federal
laws provide no exemption for those who conscientiously object on
grounds of religious belief. *Smith* itself involves yet another such law.
While some religious groups succeed in pressuring legislatures into
exempting them from burdensome laws, many do not. And the religious
groups that do not succeed are most often those that are small,
unfamiliar, and idiosyncratic in their beliefs. Yet this kind of religious
group is most in need of constitutional protection because of its relative
lack of political power.

For example, in the first unemployment compensation case, *Sherbert
v. Verner*,[20] a Seventh-Day Adventist was denied unemployment benefits
by the state of South Carolina, despite having been laid off from her job,
because she refused to accept Saturday employment. Adventists observe
a Saturday sabbath and, therefore, this worker could not work on
Saturday without violating her religious beliefs.

South Carolina did not deny benefits to unemployed Christians who
refused to accept Sunday employment, however; the unemployment
compensation law specifically provided that refusal to work on Sunday
could not be a basis for denying benefits. Since Protestants controlled
the South Carolina legislature when the law was passed, they were able
to protect themselves from being penalized for observing their sabbath
by demanding an exemption from the law.

Adventists, as a small and unfamiliar sect, had no such power, and so
the law extended no exemption to them. This is not "an unavoidable
consequence of democratic government," as the *Smith* Court apolo-
gized.[21] On the contrary, the American commitment to constitutional
government which protects basic human rights, including free exercise

of religion, suggests that the protection of such rights cannot be left to the uncertainties of majority rule. If this commitment is taken seriously, the "unavoidable consequence" is protection of powerless religious groups. Thus, in contrast to *Smith*, the Supreme Court in *Sherbert* held that South Carolina could not constitutionally penalize a worker for practicing her religion by withholding unemployment benefits.

Congress and state legislatures need not wait for the Supreme Court to act before protecting freedom of religion. The drafters and sponsors of all laws that are enacted ought to consider their impact on religion, and should include appropriate exemptive provisions when the impact is significantly adverse. A legislature that creates an exemption for politically strong religious groups shows only that it responds to power; a legislature that creates an exemption for politically powerless religious groups shows that it values religion. As with judicial exemptions, legislative exemptions send a powerful message to religious people that their communities of beliefs are valued by the larger society.

Debating whether religion is important enough to merit exemption from compliance with the law—or, alternatively, whether a law is important enough to be applied to everyone even though it burdens religious exercise—helps to develop a language that bridges the gap between religious and secular. At least as important, a country that values religion enough to undergo significant dislocation to protect it sends a positive signal to its religious citizens, reducing their disaffection and alienation by concretely illustrating the country's commitment to the truly free exercise of their enterprise. On the other hand, labeling protection of religious exercise a "luxury" that the United States can do without can only increase religious disaffection and alienation, with all their attendant dangers.

### Religion and Ethics

The 1980s saw a rebirth of unrestrained capitalism in the United States. Investigations have uncovered massive securities fraud and insider trading on Wall Street, together with incredible fraud and waste in the savings and loan industry. The crimes committed generated illegal profits that exceeded hundreds of millions of dollars, and that will cost American taxpayers billions more. A plethora of commentary on teaching business ethics has followed in the wake of these scandals. Many commentators have argued that ethics cannot be taught at all, that they are the result of a complex and subtle socialization process that cannot consciously be duplicated. Even among those who believe that ethics can be taught, many also believe that the only opportunity for such teaching is when people are young, so that it is too late to do anything about the present generation.

In the midst of the moral angst generated by the scandals of the 1980s, no one has yet mentioned making use of an obvious source of ethical teaching—religion. In Western cultures like that of the United States, ethical values often find their roots in the Judeo-Christian tradition. Moreover, as we have discussed, large numbers of people remain seriously committed to that tradition. If the very tradition from which many of our ethical principles were derived remains vital and viable, then one would think that the institutional purveyors of that tradition would be a valuable, if not indispensable, means of teaching the ethical business conduct which everyone seems to agree is lacking.

The advantages of using religion to teach ethics are clear. Many commentators have argued that ethical business conduct will take hold in a company only if its executive management consistently imposes serious sanctions on unethical conduct. This has prompted many companies to draft written "ethics codes" accompanied by warnings that violation will bring forth serious penalties. Obviously, one potential source of unethical conduct is a lack of commitment on the part of management. But even when management is committed, the code-and-sanctions approach has limitations.

Under such a system, the question whether to act ethically quickly degenerates into a sterile legalism. The code establishes itself as the minimum (and thus the only) standard employees must satisfy. Whether specific conduct is ethical or not comes to depend on close technical readings of the language of the code. Loopholes are easily found, and the code becomes either irrelevant or ever longer and more complicated in an attempt to close the loopholes. Still, many employees are deterred from unethical conduct by written ethics codes; companies that use them experience fewer ethical problems. After all, those who wish to climb the corporate ladder in such companies know that they cannot violate the code if they wish to succeed.

This apparently positive effect, however, is double-edged. The decision whether to be ethical degenerates into a calculus of personal prudence and self-interest, the advantages of disobeying the code weighed against the advantages of obeying it, all discounted by the probability of getting caught. One obeys the ethics code, not because it is morally right, but because it is smart, sort of like "dressing for success."

Contrast this with a consciously religious approach to ethics. Strong egalitarian notions pervade the New Testament, most obviously in the injunction to "love thy neighbor as thyself." Similar commands are present in the Old Testament. To those who accept the Bible as an authoritative source of morality, how these commandments are translated into contemporary life is highly relevant to the question of whether particular acts are ethical. If loving others as one's self is a divine reality of the universe, then one must be prepared to account to God for her conduct in relation to this reality. This imbues the commandment with a powerful authority over the life of one who believes in its divine origin.

One of the unquestioned attributes of the ethical person is the ability to project the consequences of a decision beyond its effect on oneself onto the community or communities to which one belongs. In other words, ethical people constantly consider the effects of their choices on others, and not just on themselves. Thus, the ethical person often forgoes a personally profitable course of action because of damage which that course might inflict upon the communities to which she belongs.

Once again, we come up against the reality that subverting one's self-interest to the good of others is difficult. People will ignore their personal interests only because of a moral vision which they share or a power they respect. Thus, businesses which attempt to teach and enforce ethics solely by creating disincentives to unethical conduct have undercut the entire enterprise. Ethical conduct demands that one think of others because others are worthy in their own right of our consideration and respect, and not because it is prudent to think of them.

Many Americans remain seriously committed to religion. Public institutions that take account of this in formulating policy avail themselves of a powerful tool. Once one ascertained the various religious preferences of a company's employees, she could formulate voluntary ethics seminars and presentations tailored to appeal to the authority of those commitments. By placing the company's policy on ethics directly within the narrative context of a religious tradition, the company enhances the possibility that the policy will be taken seriously by those who identify with the tradition. Because the otherwise disembodied urging to "be ethical" is placed within a reality which the employee believes and understands and respects, the policy is internalized to a much greater extent than when the employee is merely scared into conformity by the threat of sanctions.

When confronted with the knowledge that her religion defines certain behavior as unethical, the employee is not left with the question, "Is it in my self-interest to be ethical?" but rather, "Do I really believe in this ethical norm, and what does it mean in terms of how I conduct myself in my job?" One can talk about ethics, formulate sophisticated arguments in their favor, exhort their observance, and penalize their violation, but none of these will convince people to conduct themselves ethically as well as an appeal to the authority of a transcendent reality in which they believe. American religion is at least one source of the teaching that the value of human life is not entirely "of this world."

One of the difficulties with preaching ethics is that so often ethical conduct is not in one's immediate self-interest. Religion provides one account of the ethical life that is sufficiently powerful to challenge greed as a dominant human motivation. To the extent that it does succeed in helping people to live more ethical lives, then its insights should be welcomed in public life. In addition to being effective, the use of religion to teach ethics again places religion in a public context. Continued dialogue about the meaning of religion to the traditionally secular world of corporate business will help to create a language that bridges the gap between the religious and the secular.

Religion is a tremendous resource in addressing the difficulties and problems that confront contemporary America. Once one abandons the reflexive caricature of religion as an irrational and destabilizing enterprise, it becomes possible plausibly to conceive of religion—of religious knowledge—as contributing to the public dialogue on how best to confront the complexities of contemporary American life. Pluralizing public life by adding religious knowledge to the secular knowledge that is already there enables a broader and more effective approach to these problems.

## RELIGION AND RESPONSIBILITY IN PUBLIC LIFE

We have argued that it is oppressive and dangerous to establish and maintain a wholly secular public culture in the United States. It would be at least as oppressive and dangerous to establish and maintain a wholly religious public culture—a theocracy. If religious people and organizations ought to be able to participate fully in American public life without shedding or disguising their religious identity, as we have argued, then in a postsecular society, secularists and others without a religious orientation should be granted the same privilege of participating in public life without abandoning their personal (nonreligious) identities. Religion needs to exercise caution and sensitivity in positions of public influence so as not to use those positions to stifle and harass the voices of those who disagree with them, even when the voices belong (God forbid!) to "secular humanists."

Unfortunately, many religious individuals and groups have shown little inclination to be cautious or sensitive in their public interactions with those of differing views. Some sense of this may lie beneath the Supreme Court's actual disposition of the case in *Bowen v. Kendrick*, which we discussed in Chapter 11. The *Bowen* Court refused to issue a blanket ruling that the Act was constitutional in all facts and circumstances; it left open the possibility that the manner in which funds are used under the Act might render it unconstitutional in particular situations. Indeed it is probably safe to assume that some religious recipients of aid under the Act were not satisfied with using that assistance to counsel only teens who make an informed choice to listen to their particular religious viewpoint on teenage sex and pregnancy. There is a real danger that some religious groups will use the wedge of public recognition and assistance provided by the Act to proselytize and coerce religious belief among adolescents who do not share (and who do not wish to consider adopting) the groups' religious premises.

The quest for power and control by religious groups has been a recurrent theme in Western history. In fact, the interests of institutional religion have often opposed those who have had the most powerful religious experiences. Joan of Arc, for example, was put to death primarily because of her refusal to subordinate the reality of her personal religious experiences to the authority of the medieval church.

Joan surfaced in the 15th century in the midst of the Hundred Years' War between the English and the French over succession to the French crown. She had had numerous experiences in which God communicated with her through the voices of Saint Michael, Saint Catherine, and Saint Margaret. Confident of divine guidance, she presented herself to the Dauphin, the French claimant to the throne, offering her assistance to his cause. The Dauphin sent her to Orleans, where Joan roused the French to an attack on the ring of English forts surrounding the city. Her battle decisions consistently revealed knowledge of the strength and situation of the English that was available to no one else. The English retreated from Orleans within a week. Over the next few months, she led the French to victory after victory, leading to the assumption of the crown by the Dauphin with Joan at his side. After every battle, she attributed her success to the voices of the saints.

The English captured Joan while she was attempting to relieve the siege of yet another French city, but the French made no attempt to rescue or ransom her. She was eventually tried by the Inquisition for heresy on account of her claim to direct revelation outside of the channels sanctioned by the church. After months of relentless questioning, having been repeatedly threatened with death by fire, she agreed to renounce her revelations as evil and submit to the exclusive authority of the church to interpret them.

Within days, however, she reaffirmed the validity of her religious experiences, boldly stating that she had repented of the treason of denying them. She was burned for heresy May 30, 1431. The verdict of heresy was revoked in 1450, largely for political reasons, but Joan was never cleared of the charge that she usurped the authority of the church by interpreting her own revelations. Unable to convince Joan that only its hierarchy rightfully could communicate with God, the church simply silenced her.[22]

The story of Joan is more relevant to contemporary religion than one might initially think. Consider the controversy several years ago over Martin Scorsese's movie, "The Last Temptation of Christ." (Part of this controversy was no doubt orchestrated by movie distributors anxious to sell tickets. Nevertheless, there is an aspect to it that bears on our point.) Taking seriously the Christian belief that Jesus was both God and man, Scorsese sought to portray the human as well as the divine Jesus. Given the traditional Christian emphasis on Jesus's divine nature, Scorsese chose to highlight his human nature in the film. Against the backdrop of divine myth, the placement of human attributes like cowardice, vulgarity, and lust in the life of Jesus—even as mere temptations—seemed jarring and blasphemous to many Christians. Numerous churches condemned the movie, and many of these sought to exercise their political and economic power to prevent the movie from being shown.

In contrast to a secular public life, which requires that people disguise or abandon religious beliefs and experiences when acting in public, Scorsese's movie was attacked because it abandoned—or, at least, radically reinterpreted—the conventional religious myth of Jesus. In the view of those who protested the movie, Jesus must be discussed in the traditional language of the sacred or not at all. One must wonder, if such people were in control of American public life, whether they would let any nonreligious voice into the public square.

Many religious groups, especially fundamentalist ones, seem to have forgotten that contemporary religion owes much to the humanistic influences of the Renaissance, the Reformation, and the Enlightenment. Many churches and religious people seem untroubled by the thought that public life might be dominated and controlled by a particular view of the world; they are troubled only because a worldview other than their own is dominating and controlling.

They do not believe it is wrong for one perception of human reality to force out all others, so long as the victorious perception is the particular one they espouse. Thus, they assent to the basic assumptions of a secular public life in America; they differ only in asserting that the sacred rather than the secular should be the prerequisite for participation in public life. Rather than moving from a modern to a postmodern world, they would regress from modernism to medievalism.

If discarding the metaphor of separation and transcending the various dualisms it implies requires that religion as religion be accorded a legitimate place in public life, as we have argued, one must also acknowledge the great responsibility this places on religious people and groups. They must resist the temptation to use public acceptance, recognition, and legitimation to sacralize American public life.

If religion casts secularism out of the temple of public life and replaces it with religion, the entire cycle of alienation, abandonment, and revolution will be repeated, only this time by secularists. At a time when the news remains filled with stories of religious leaders advocating violence against those with whom they disagree, the risk that secular domination of public life could be replaced with religious domination is not one lightly to be dismissed.

## RELIGION AND RELEVANCE TO PUBLIC LIFE

There is a further challenge in public religious zeal even if religious domination of public life is avoided. This threat is to religion itself. To remain vital and viable in a postmodern world, religion must continue to be relevant to life in such a world. As we have argued, the ultimate criterion by which one can rationally evaluate a religious experience is whether or not it "works"—whether or not the knowledge imparted by the experience helps one to flourish, to live the most satisfying life of which she can conceive, given the situation in which she finds herself. Religions that are deemed impediments to a better life may well be abandoned and simply fail to survive as viable lifestyle choices.

Religious institutions that wish to survive in this kind of world will most likely reconsider their relationship to their believers. One of the persistent claims of Western religion has been access to Truth, and the relationship of a believer to her church and her religion has traditionally been defined by some claim of the religion to Truth. People were attracted to a religion, and remained loyal to it, primarily because of a witness or intuition or habit of thought which characterized their religion as the one that most accurately represented God, the Reality with which all humans must ultimately come to terms. In this respect, the claims of religion have mirrored the correspondence theory of truth which has dominated Western thinking for centuries. That religion was "true" which most closely corresponded to the divine presence.

In a postmodern world, truth as correspondence is not an adequate account of how people live; they also need a concept like flourishing to measure truth (including religious truth). Postmodern believers will become more focused on how well their church helps them to live. As well as believing that their religion helps them to live well because it corresponds to divine will, religious people in a postmodern world will believe that their religion corresponds to divine will because it helps them to live well. Whether a church does indeed help its members to live rich, satisfying, fulfilling lives will become at least as important as its claim to exclusive spiritual authority.

Postmodernism also suggests the possibility that religions may alter their relationship with one another, as well as with their believers. For centuries, the medieval church exercised a monopoly on access to Truth in the Western world. The Reformation dissolved that monopoly, but not the idea of Truth. We now have religious pluralism, especially in the United States, but in general each religion still claims that it is the exclusive vehicle for accessing Reality.

An emphasis on pragmatism, on discovering what helps one to live well, is likely to point religions in a more collaborative direction. Discussions about religious truth in a postmodern world will be centered more on what works than on what corresponds. In this kind of world, other religions become resources for insights and ideas about ways to live a fulfilling life, rather than theological competitors. For example, if American Catholics work out an effective approach to preventing teen pregnancy by teaching abstinence from premarital sex, the approach will be considered by other religions as well. The effectiveness of a solution to a serious social problem will almost certainly outweigh suspicion about the source of the problem. An era of institutional competition among religions is fading; an era of institutional cooperation approaches.

In one sense postmodernism is good news for religion, foreshadowing the end of the secular monopoly on public life, and on knowledge generally. In another sense, however, postmodernism challenges religion by undermining its traditional claim to Truth. The arguments that we have directed at secularism's exclusion of religion from public life can also be turned against religion itself.

Thus, the aftermath of the secular society will be a challenging time for religious institutions and individuals. They are likely simultaneously to experience both exhilarating liberation from the constraints of secularism and deep insecurity about the postmodern challenge to their religious understanding of themselves. Many believers may find themselves in the ironic position of believing in the overwhelming Truth of their compelling religious experience while also acknowledging the force of the postmodern critique.

It is worth remembering that times of conflict, contradiction, and even chaos present creative opportunities as well as destructive threats. "Without Contraries there is no progression," wrote the Romantic poet William Blake.[23] Indeed, without opposition, there may well be no meaningful human existence at all.[24] In the long run, those religious institutions and individuals that attempt to understand and to live with the conflict between exclusive Truth and postmodern pragmatism will strengthen themselves. In the struggle with postmodernism they will uncover greater insights about the meaning and application of their religious beliefs. Consequently, in meeting the needs of their members and in influencing the society in which they find themselves, they will almost certainly be more effective than those who refuse to confront the conflict.

## NOTES

1. Milner Ball, *Lying Down Together: Law, Metaphor and Theology* (Madison: University of Wisconsin Press, 1985), 42. See also ibid., 45; Richard John Neuhaus, *The Naked Public Square: Religion and Democracy in America*, 2d ed. (Grand Rapids, Mich.: Eerdmans, 1986), 112.

2. Ball, *Lying Down Together*, ch. 3.

3. Michael J. Perry, *Love and Power: The Proper Role of Religion and Morality in American Politics* (New York: Oxford University Press, [forthcoming] 1991); Michael J. Perry, *Morality, Politics and Law* (New York: Oxford University Press, 1988), ch. 6.

4. Ball, *Lying Down Together*, chapt. 6

5. Luke 7.1–10 (New English Bible).

6. Nikos Kazantzakis, *The Last Temptation of Christ*, trans. P. A. Bien (New York: Bantam 1960), 380.

7. Joseph Campbell, *The Power of Myth*, ed. Betty Sue Flowers (New York: Doubleday, 1988), 61.

8. 482 U.S. 578 (1987).

9. E.g., Gregory Gelfand, "Of Monkeys and Men—An Atheist's Heretical View of the Constitutionality of Teaching the Disproof of a Religion in the Public Schools,"

*Journal of Law and Education* 16 (1987): 271; Symposium, "Creationism v. Evolution: Radical Perspectives on the Confrontation of Spirit and Science," *Tikkun* (Nov./Dec. 1987): 55.

10. 482 U.S. 578, 592 (1987).

11. Ibid., 634 (dissenting opinion) (citation omitted).

12. 487 U.S. 589 (1988).

13. See Coleman, "Classroom Sex Ed Alone Has Little Impact on Teen Sex Behavior," *Macon Telegraph & News* (March 2, 1989): 1 (Associated Press story).

14. Perry, *Morality, Politics, and Law*, 10–20.

15. "Tackling Difficult Issues: Panel Discusses Religion and the Public Schools," *Law Quadrangle Notes* (Fall 1988): 10, 11.

16. 110 S.Ct. 1595 (1990).

17. Ibid., 1605 (emphasis in original).

18. Ibid., 1616 (Blackmun, J., dissenting).

19. Ibid., 1606.

20. 374 U.S. 398 (1963).

21. 110 S.Ct. 1595, 1606 (1990).

22. For a chronology of Joan's life, see *The First Biography of Joan of Arc, With the Chronicle Record of a Contemporary Account*, trans. & annot. Daniel Rankin and Claire Quintal (Pittsburgh: University of Pittsburgh Press, 1964).

23. Quoted in Hazard Adams, *Antithetical Essays in Literary Criticism and Liberal Education* (Tallahassee: Florida State University Press, 1990), 5. For discussions of this use of irony by the Romantic poets, see Hazard Adams, "The Dizziness of Freedom; or, Why I Read William Blake," in ibid., 3–17; Neil M. Flax, "Goethe and Romanticism," in *Approaches to Teaching Goethe's Faust*, ed. Douglas J. McMillan (New York: Modern Language Association of America, 1987), 40–47.

24. Cf. *The Book of Mormon* (Salt Lake City, Utah: The Church of Jesus Christ of Latter-Day Saints, 1981) (original ed. 1830), 2 Nephi 2.11–13 ("For it must needs be, that there is an opposition in all things. If not so. . . , all things must have vanished away.").

# Conclusion: The Future of Religion

The United States is and will continue to be a country with a strong religious component to its culture. Throughout the 20th century Americans have remained among the most religious people in the world, and all the available data suggest that religion will continue to command the allegiance of millions of Americans in the foreseeable future. Although in recent decades American religiosity has largely been confined to private life, it is increasingly asserting itself in public life as well. To the extent that any change occurs in the level of religious commitment in the United States, it almost certainly will be in the direction of more rather than less religious belief, with more expansive rather than more narrow applications and assertions of such beliefs. Participants in American public life must reconcile themselves to the fact that the secularization hypothesis is false. Religion is in America to stay.

In at least one respect, the persistence of religion in the United States is unsurprising, for American religion has historically helped its believers to meet personal needs, and it continues to do so today. For those many Americans who want to improve both themselves and their society, religion remains an important resource. Indeed, when considered in light of the failures of secularism in fully meeting the needs of individuals and of society during the 20th century, the resources of religion seem virtually indispensable.

Nevertheless, it is unlikely that religion and religious belief will re-enter American public life without a struggle. The public secularism that has characterized the 20th century in the United States is deeply threatened by the participation of religion in public life. A sharp and potentially violent confrontation is inevitable between the largely secular institutions of government and other components of public life, on the one hand, and radical and not-so-radical groups of believers, on the other. As we have argued, we believe that ultimately the United States will resolve this conflict by accomodating religion in public life rather than continuing to confine it within the limits of private life.

The acceptance of religion into public life as a legitimate and valued participant will foster the creation of a different language of public life. Secular ideas and concepts will no longer predominate; instead, the language of public life will evolve in a way that will enable people genuinely and authentically to express their deepest religious sentiments and aspirations in public contexts. As a result, religion will cease to be judged in public life according to exclusively secular criteria drawn from history, psychology, sociology, and other such secular disciplines. The most important evaluative criterion in judging the personal and social value of religion will instead be functional and pragmatic: how well does a particular religion or religious belief help its members to flourish as human beings, to live the freest, most responsible, most productive, most honest, most peaceful, and most satisfying lives of which they are capable?

With the emphasis on ways of becoming better people and a better society, we may hope for more cooperation and less competition, not only between secular groups and religious groups, but also between the churches and other religious groups themselves. Living well in the contemporary world is an immense and complex challenge; it will require every insight that can be gleaned from the ever-increasing store of human knowledge, be it secular, religious, or (even) sectarian. To the post modern believer, the source of knowledge is far less important than its usefulness. Just as religion in general has much of value to add to the secular account of human existence, each particular religion is a source of potentially valuable insights about human living for other religions.

The need to change the public dynamic from competition to cooperation has been dramatically underlined by the resurgence of Islam around the world in recent years. As secular government structures have fallen—in particular those of the Soviet Union—fundamentalist Muslims have moved to fill the resultant political and social vacuums. It is at least possible, if not likely, that the dominant challenge to the western world in the immediate future will come from fundamentalist Islam. Muslims who are struggling with and resisting the inroads of western science and technology will find little to recommend the current secularization of American public life. Likewise, an America that is committed to secularized public life is ill-equipped to understand and influence a Muslim society in which religion penetrates to every aspect of individual and social life. Thus, the key to dealing with the coming Islamic challenge could well be found in the manner in which religion comes to be accepted in American public life and cooperation comes to replace competition among secular and religious groups.

For all these reasons, we have argued that American public life in a postmodern age must include religion as a legitimate participant. There can be no mistaking the difficulty of this task, requiring as it will strange new habits of citizenship in the public square. At the same time, there can be no avoiding the conclusion that continued exclusion of religious speech from public life is simply an arbitrary exercise of power.

The religious traditions of the West have persisted through more than three millennia because they work—they help large numbers of people to live well. The Biblical narrative preserves and communicates a deep human wisdom.[1] We ought to consider this wisdom in our political and social deliberations because, as law professor John Garvey has written, "religion is important," and "God is good."[2] Religion should not be pushed to the margins of public life, but rather should take its place alongside nonreligious disciplines in the "real" world of knowledge

The prospect of a greater role for religion in public life along the lines that we have sketched is likely to trouble many Americans, religious and nonreligious alike. Yet reconciling public life to the beliefs of religious Americans potentially benefits all Americans. Alienation and radicalization of religion lead to persistent challenging and rethinking of basic church–state assumptions. Moreover, increasingly frequent incursions of government into religious life and the continued hostility of public culture towards religion place religious people and institutions in a reflexive, defensive posture. In this frame of mind, religious groups and individuals resist even reasonable government regulations, and ignore the valid criticisms and insights of outsiders.

A person can compromise politically only when she believes that her political rights are not at risk. "Assurance that rights are secure tends to diminish fear and jealousy of strong government, and by making us feel safe to live under it makes for its better support."[3] From accommodation and de-radicalization of the religious population of the United States could flow less strident assertions of religion in public life. Secure in the knowledge that religion is acceptable in public as well as private life, religious Americans could become less defensive about both government regulation and secular influences in public life. Ultimately, one may hope for an American public life that accepts religion but remains as open and tolerant as the ideal society imagined in the American dream of political freedom and equality.

Religious people must realize in their turn that just as a public life dominated by secularism alienates and radicalizes religious people, a public life dominated by religion will alienate and radicalize secularists. The current state of affairs privileges secular discourse in public life and disables religious discourse. It is no improvement to privilege religion and disable secularism. Avoiding this will require the exercise of considerable responsibility and restraint by religious groups and individuals to ensure that they do not rely on their access to public life as an excuse to dominate public life. "Those who claim the right to influence," states the Williamsburg Charter, "should accept the responsibility not to inflame."[4]

In the end, even if it is freely admitted to public life, religion must come to grips with why it wants to participate in that life. Imposing a religious ideology on American public life is merely to exchange secular criteria of legitimacy for religious ones. Believers become the privileged insiders, secularists become the alienated outsiders, and the nature of the conflict—the arbitrary imposition of power—remains the same.

If the point of religious participation in public life is to suppress competing conceptions of the world, then our argument for such participation has been for naught. If Western religion has worked for three thousand years, then surely Western knowledge has worked for at least three hundred—indeed, it has succeeded beyond anyone's wildest dreams. God is good, but so is science; it, too, has helped many people to live their lives well. As Einstein so aptly stated, "Religion without science is blind. Science without religion is lame."[5] In reaching beyond secularism, one must take care not to destroy it, for religion cannot take its place alongside secularism as a legitimate public discourse unless secularism remains a legitimate discourse as well.

Thus, the future of religion is in its own hands. If religion adopts a public role which assumes that it, and only it, has access to Truth and Reality, religion will not meet the deepest needs and aspirations of its believers. At best, it will merely continue the cycle of alienation and cultural oppression begun by secularism; at worst, it will disappear. If, on the other hand, religion chooses a role in American public life which emphasizes tolerance and cooperation with other public actors in the never-ending human search for the most satisfying and fulfilling way to live one's life, it will itself flourish: it will help both believers and nonbelievers to choose the dream.

# NOTES

1. Michael J. Perry, *Love and Power: The Proper Role of Religion and Morality in American Politics* (New York: Oxford University Press, [forthcoming] 1991).

2. John H. Garvey, *God is Good* (unpub. ms., 1990), 1; cf. Harold Berman, *The Interaction of Law and Religion* (Nashville, Tenn.: Abingdon, 1974), 75 ("We must recognize that the great passions which created our [religious] heritage also create a presumption in favor of preserving it.").

3. West Virginia Board of Education v. Barnett, 319 U.S. 624, 636–37 (1943).

4. *The Williamsburg Charter* (Williamsburg, Va.: n.p., 1988), 21.

5. Quoted in Paul Davies, *God and the New Physics* (New York: Simon & Schuster, 1983), epigraph.

# Select Bibliography

For those who wish to pursue these issues further, we have listed here the primary sources on which we relied in writing this book. However, this list is not a complete compilation of all of the sources we consulted.

## BOOKS

Adams, Hazard. "Canons: Literary Criteria/Power Criteria." In *Antithetical Essays in Literary Criticism and Liberal Education*, 166–83. Tallahassee: Florida State University Press, 1990.

_____. "Neo-Blakean Prolegomena to an Unlikely Academic Structure." In *Antithetical Essays in Literary Criticism and Liberal Education*, 272–87. Tallahassee: Florida State University Press, 1990.

Ashley, Maurice. *England in the Seventeenth Century*. 3d ed. New York: Barnes & Noble, 1967.

Association for Supervision and Curriculum Development. *Religion in the Curriculum: A Report from the ASCD Panel on Religion in the Curriculum*. Alexandria, Va.: Association for Supervision and Curriculum Development, 1987.

Bainton, Roland H. *The Reformation of the 16th Century*. London: Hodder & Staughton, 1953.

Ball, Milner. *Lying Down Together: Law, Metaphor, and Theology*. Madison: University of Wisconsin Press, 1985.

Bellah, Robert N. *The Broken Covenant: American Civil Religion in Time of Trial*. New York: Seabury, 1975.

Berman, Harold. *The Interaction of Law and Religion*. Nashville, Tenn.: Abingdon, 1974.

_____. *Law and Revolution*. Cambridge: Harvard University Press, 1983.

Campbell, Joseph. *The Power of Myth*. Edited by Betty Sue Flowers. New York: Doubleday, 1988.

_____, ed. *Myths, Dreams, and Religion*. New York: Dutton, 1970.

Capra, Fritjof. *The Tao of Physics: An Exploration of the Parallels Between Modern Physics and Eastern Meditation*. 2d ed., revised and updated. Boston: New Science, 1985.

Clark, George Norman. *The Seventeenth Century*. 2d ed. Oxford: Clarendon, 1947.

Curry, Thomas. *The First Freedoms: Church and State in America to the Passage of the First Amendment*. New York: Oxford University Press, 1986.

Davies, Paul. *God and the New Physics*. New York: Simon and Schuster, 1983.

Eagleton, Terry. *Literary Theory: An Introduction*. Minneapolis: University of Minnesota Press, 1983.

Eliade, Mircea. *The Sacred and the Profane: The Nature of Religion*. Translated by Willard R. Trask. New York: Harcourt Brace Jovanovich, 1959.

_____, ed.-in-chief. *The Encyclopedia of Religion*. 16 vols. New York: Macmillan, 1987.

Erikson, Erik H. *Childhood and Society*. 2d ed. New York: Norton, 1963.

Frankl, Viktor. *Man's Search for Meaning: An Introduction to Logotherapy*. Translated by Ilse Lasch. Boston: Beacon, 1959.

Garraty, John A., and Peter Gay. *The Columbia History of the World*. New York: Harper & Row, 1972.

Greenawalt, Kent. *Religious Convictions and Political Choice*. New York: Oxford University Press, 1988.

Guntrip, Harry. *Psychoanalytic Theory, Therapy, and the Self*. New York: Basic, 1971.

Hallett, Garth L. *Language and Truth*. New Haven: Yale University Press, 1988.

Hauerwas, Stanley. *A Community of Character*. Notre Dame, Ind.: Notre Dame University Press, 1981.

Howe, Mark De Wolfe. *The Garden and the Wilderness*. Chicago: University of Chicago Press, 1965.

Jung, Carl G. *Analytical Psychology: Its Theory and Practice*. 1st American ed. New York: Pantheon, 1968.

_____. "Approaching the Unconscious." In *Man and His Symbols*, edited by Carl G. Jung, 1–94. New York: Dell, 1968.

_____. *The Portable Jung*. Edited by Joseph Campbell, translated by Ronald Hull. New York: Penguin, 1976.

Kelley, Dean, ed. *Government Intervention in Religious Affairs*. New York: Pilgrim, 1982.

Kuhn, Thomas. *The Structure of Scientific Revolutions*. 2d ed. Berkeley: University of California Press, 1970.

Kung, Hans. *On Being a Christian*. Translated by Edward Quinn. New York: Doubleday, 1976.

Lindsay, A. *Religion, Science, and Society in the Modern World*. New Haven: Yale University Press, 1943.

MacIntyre, Alasdair. *A Short History of Ethics*. New York: Macmillan, 1966.

Neuhaus, Richard John. *The Naked Public Square: Religion and Democracy in America*. 2d ed. Grand Rapids, Mich.: Eerdmans, 1986.

Ortega y Gassett, José. "Concord and Liberty." In *Concord and Liberty*, translated by Helene Weyl, 9–47. New York: Norton, 1946.

Perry, Michael J. *Morality, Politics, and Law: A Bicenntential Essay*. New York: Oxford University Press, 1988.

_____. *Love and Power: The Proper Role of Religion and Morality in American Politics*. New York: Oxford University Press, [forthcoming] 1991.

Purcell, Edward A., Jr. *The Crisis of Democratic Theory: Scientific Naturalism and the Problem of Value*. Lexington: University Press of Kentucky, 1973.

Reichley, A. James. *Religion in American Public Life*. Washington, D.C.: Brookings Institute, 1985.

Rockefeller Foundation. *The Religion Beat: The Reporting of Religion in the Media*. Conference Report. New York: Rockefeller, 1981.

Russell, Bertrand. *Religion and Science*. New York: Oxford University Press, 1961.

Sabine, George. *A History of Political Theory*. Rev. ed. New York: Holt, Rinehart & Winston, 1950.

Smith, Rogers. *Liberalism and American Constitutional Law*. New Haven: Yale University Press, 1985.

Tillich, Paul. *Theology of Culture*. Edited by Robert C. Kimball. New York: Oxford University Press, 1978.

Tushnet, Mark V. *Red, White, and Blue: A Critical Analysis of Constitutional Law*. Cambridge: Harvard University Press, 1988.

Unger, Roberto Mangabeira. *Knowledge and Politics*. New York: Free, 1975.

Vitz, Paul. *Religion and Traditional Values in Public School Textbooks: An Empirical Study*. Washington, D.C.: National Institute of Education, 1985.

*The Williamsburg Charter*. Williamsburg, Va.: n.p., 1988.

## ARTICLES

Adams, Arlin, and Charles Emmerich. "A Heritage of Religious Liberty." *University of Pennsylvania Law Review* 137 (1989): 1559–671.

Berger, Peter. "Religion in Post-Protestant America." *Commentary* 81 (May 1986): 41–46.

Berman, Harold. "Religion and Law: The First Amendment in Political Perspective." *Emory Law Journal* 35 (1986): 777–97.

Bradley, Gerard V. "Dogmatomachy—A 'Privatization' Theory of the Religion Clause Cases." *Saint Louis University Law Journal* 30 (1986): 275–330.

_____. "The No Religious Test Clause and the Constitution of Religious Liberty: A Machine That Has Gone of Itself." *Case Western Reserve Law Review* (1987): 674–747.

Cover, Robert. "The Supreme Court, 1982 Term—Foreward: *Nomos* and Narrative." *Harvard Law Review* 97 (1983): 4–68.

Edmundson, Mark. "A Will to Cultural Power: Deconstructing the DeMan Scandal." *Harper's Magazine* 277 (July 1988): 67–71.

_____. "Prophet of a New Post-Modernism: The Greater Challenge of Salman Rushdie." *Harper's Magazine* 279 (Dec. 1989): 62–71.

Frug, Gerald. "The City as a Legal Concept." *Harvard Law Review* 93 (1980): 1059–154.

Garet, Ronald. "Communality and Existence: The Rights of Groups." *Southern California Law Review* 56 (1983): 1002–75.

Hutchinson, Allan C. and Patrick J. Monahan, "The 'Rights' Stuff: Roberto Unger and Beyond." *Texas Law Review* 62 (1984): 1477–539.

Karst, Kenneth. "The Freedom of Intimate Association." *Yale Law Journal* 89 (1980): 624–92.

_____. "Paths to Belonging: The Constitution and Cultural Identity." *North Carolina Law Review* 64 (1986): 303–77.

MacNeil, Ian. "Bureaucracy, Liberalism, and Community—American Style." *Northwestern University Law Review* 79 (1985): 900–48.

Ozick, Cynthia. "The Moral Necessity of Metaphor." *Harper's Magazine* 272 (May 1986): 62–68.

Peller, Gary. "Reason and the Mob: The Politics of Representation." *Tikkun* 2 (no. 3): 28–31, 92–95.

Putnam, Ruth Anna. "Creating Facts and Values." *Philosophy* 60 (1985): 187–204.

Smith, Geoffrey. "The Special Place of Religion in the Constitution." *Supreme Court Review* 1983: 83–123.

Smith, Steven D. "The Restoration of Tolerance." *California Law Review* 78 (1990): 305–56.

_____. "Separation and the Secular: Reconstructing the Disestablishment Decision." *Texas Law Review* 67 (1989): 955–1031.

# Index

Hobbes, Thomas, 27, 140–41, 144. *See also* Enlightenment; Liberalism

Holocaust, 88, 106, 156. *See also* Judaism

Hostility to religion, 4, 11–18, 29–30, 59–60, 63–65, 71–77, 82–83, 92–93. *See also* Enlightenment; Public life; Secularism

Humanism, 18, 82, 94, 175, 176

Individualism, 75, 93–94, 143, 149–52, 154–55, 166; autonomy, 27. *See also* Liberalism

Islam, 5, 13, 22, 30, 111; contemporary influence of, 109, 135, 182–83; holy war, 140; Muhammad and origin of, 13, 109; progressive elements of, 134, 140

Jackson, Jesse, 139

Japanese Americans, internment of, 89–90

Jaynes, Julian, 64

Jefferson, Thomas, 42, 141–42, 160–61

Jesus, 54, 58–59, 110, 111, 129, 162–63, 171

Joan of Arc, 13, 64, 175–76

Judaism, 5, 22, 43, 69, 86, 111, 167; holocaust of, 88, 106, 156; Judeo-Christian tradition, 100, 134, 151–52, 162; Moses and origin of, 107–8; social contributions of, 13, 139

Judeo-Christian tradition, 100, 134, 151–52, 172

Judges, secular orientation of, 66–69

Jung, Carl G., 51–61 *passim*, 74; archetypes, 56–61, 74; collective unconscious, 56–61

Kazantzakis, Nikos, 162

King, Martin Luther, Jr., 101, 140

Kuhn, Thomas, 128

Langdell, Christopher Columbus, 65

*The Last Temptation of Christ* (Kazantzakis), 162–63

*The Last Temptation of Christ* (Scorsese), 176

Legal realists, 65

Legitimacy of religion in public life, 31–32, 101–2, 112–13, 130, 139–79

Liberalism, 3, 27, 82–83, 94; antinomial nature of, 27–28, 161; focus of, on self-interest, 26–27, 155, 166–67, 172–74; groups and, 147, 155; Hobbes, Thomas, 27, 140–41, 144; moral neutrality of, 22–23, 25, 88–89, 143–44, 151; privatization of religion and, 26–30, 86–87, 140–42; relation with secularism, 86–87; stages of, 87–88; threat of, to individual freedom, 140–43, 145. *See also* Enlightenment; Individualism; Secularism

Lindsay, A. D., 144

Luther, Martin, 39, 136

*Lynch v. Donnelly*, 20 n.24

*Lyng v. Northwest Indian Cemetery Association*, 67–68

*McCollum v. Board of Education*, 19 n.10

McConnell, Michael, 49 n.9.

MacIntyre, Alasdair, 39

Madison, James, 141

*Marsh v. Chambers*, 20 n.24

Marty, Martin, 31–32

Marxism, 47–48, 59; Soviet Union, 10, 89–90, 136, 144, 182

Modernism, 59–60, 129; antipathy of, to religion, 64–65, 87–88; religious reactions to, 71–77, 176–771; secular character of, 100–112, 130, 136–37; threat of, to individual freedom, 140–45, 147–52. *See also* Enlightenment; Liberalism; Postmodernism; Science; Secularism

Mormonism, 5, 13, 86; The Book of Mormon, 110, 174 n.25; *The Polygamy Cases*, 44, 69; Smith, Joseph and origin of, 110–11

Moses, 107–8

MOVE, 90–91

Muhammad, 13, 109

## About the Authors

FREDERICK MARK GEDICKS is Professor of Law at Brigham Young University. He has contributed numerous articles to legal periodicals, including the *Southern California Law Review* and the *Wisconsin Law Review.*

ROGER HENDRIX is president of the Hendrix Information Group, Inc., a management consulting firm based in Los Angeles. He is the co-author of *Leverage Point*, a lecturer and radio commentator on social, political and economic issues, and the author of numerous articles relating to religious education.